Praise for *UDL and Ble*

Katie Novak and Catlin Tucker take
learning adventure in the book *UDL a*
a perfect mix of practical tips and solid theory, they give a road
map for blended learning no matter what barriers the learning
environment presents. Whether you are new to the world of
blended learning with UDL or could teach a course on both, this
book is sure to set you ablaze with new ideas to reach and teach
with equity in mind for all learners.

> **—Andratesha Fritzgerald,** author of *Anti-Racism and Universal
> Design for Learning: Building Expressways for Success*

A compelling must-read! In this dynamic partnership, Novak and
Tucker bring UDL and blended learning together in a fresh way
that is inspiring, accessible, and actionable. With empathy and
respect, they clearly articulate the mindset, models, strategies, and
relationships necessary for students to thrive as expert learners.
This book is a gift to all educators and those they serve. If you are
ready to leverage the power of UDL to design blended learning
that meets the needs of ALL learners, this book is required reading.

> **—Lainie Rowell,** lead author of *Evolving Learner* and contributor
> to the 2019 National Standards for Quality Online Teaching

When two leading voices on Universal Design for Learning (UDL)
and blended learning join forces, the whole is greater than the
parts. Indeed, Katie Novak and Catlin Tucker have produced an
important and timely book. Novak and Tucker point out that
UDL and BL do not simply specify techniques that teachers can
"do"—both reflect more fundamental beliefs about holding high
expectations for *all* learners while providing multiple and flexible
pathways for helping students meet them. If you care about giving
students more flexibility to personalize their learning through a
blend of in-person and online environments, you'll want this book.

> **—Jay McTighe,** educational consultant and co-author
> of the Understanding by Design® framework

This is a must-have book! The authors brilliantly (and through an engaging writing style with great stories and visuals) take you through how to design teaching and learning through the lens of UDL and blended learning. This book will support you as you create pathways for students to be more effective learners. You'll also find that you have gained strategies for your tool kit to better connect with learners in a meaningful and authentic way.

—**Nathan Lang-Raad,** consultant, speaker, and author
of five books, including *Everyday Instructional
Coaching* and *The Teachers of Oz*

We know every learner has different strengths, talents, and challenges. Instead of teaching to the mythical average learner, it's time to design learning experiences to meet each learner where they are. In this must-read book, Katie Novak and Catlin Tucker team up to synthesize the UDL and blended learning frameworks to provide educators with a roadmap to navigate the future of education. Throughout this book, you will learn strategies that will help you remove barriers to powerful learning, create more personalized learning experiences, and teach students how to become expert learners. This is a book every teacher needs to read.

—**Katie Martin, Ph.D.,** chief impact officer at Altitude
Learning and author of *Learner-Centered Innovation*

Novak and Tucker have written a delightfully engaging book about the intersections of UDL and learning technologies. From date nights to duck boats, from pigeon racing to pizza delivery, from crossword puzzles to paper dolls, they bring their respective expertise together in a way that is incredibly powerful and immensely practical. *UDL and Blended Learning* is packed with thoughtful, actionable ideas and structures. Whether you're a classroom teacher, instructional coach, or principal, this instructional design book will occupy prime territory on your favorite bookshelf.

—**Dr. Scott McLeod,** associate professor at the University
of Colorado Denver, and founding director of CASTLE

How do we prepare students for their future, rather than our past? Building on years of personal, professional and practical experience, Dr. Catlin Tucker and Dr. Katie Novak invite the reader to engage in collaborative discussions that provide essential questions and connections to the issues that education is currently facing, as well as some insight into how to prepare all learners for a complex, equitable, and interconnected future. The authors help educators understand how to embrace technology, variability, and diversity where high expectations, relationships, and personalized pathways serve as the guideposts for where we are going and, more importantly, how we will get there.

—**Maria S. Hersey, Ph.D.,** principal advisor,
Global Education Advisors

Katie Novak and Catlin Tucker offer strategies for supporting students in this time of great change in education, but these same practices will not go out of style as education continues to shift and adapt to new realities. Their blending of personal stories and concrete strategies for teachers makes this book both enjoyable and practical. Every teacher who cares about equity—who wants to offer a rich and robust educational experience to all of their students—needs to read this book!

—**Mike Anderson,** education consultant and author
of *Learning to Choose, Choosing to Learn*

UDL and Blended Learning offers a blueprint for the future of education where reactive adaptations are replaced by an equitable, proactive approach and an unwavering belief that all students can reach sophisticated learning goals, a future where learners are authentic partners in determining what those goals are to begin with. Packed with theoretical foundations, practical strategies, relevant and timely topics, and fun anecdotes, Novak and Tucker invite readers to reimagine what's possible for a twenty-first-century classroom. This book should be studied by teachers, administrators, and all other stakeholders.

—**Tom Schimmer,** author, speaker, and consultant

UDL and Blended Learning is centered around what matters in education: meeting the students where they are, providing flexibility, removing barriers, and instilling empowerment. Dr. Novak and Dr. Tucker provide practical guidance that any educator can apply to their courses. Whether you are a teacher, a professor, or an instructional designer, this book can and will help you create a more meaningful learning experience for your students.

—Luke Hobson, EdD, Program Manager at
Massachusetts Institute of Technology

UDL and Blended Learning

Katie Novak & Catlin R. Tucker

UDL

and

Blended Learning

Thriving in
Flexible
Learning
Landscapes

UDL and Blended Learning: Thriving in Flexible Learning Landscapes
© 2021 Katie Novak & Catlin Tucker

This book is available at special discounts when purchased in quantity for use as premiums, promotions, fundraisers, or for educational use. For inquiries and details, contact the publisher at books@impressbooks.org.

Published by IMpress, a division of Dave Burgess Consulting, Inc.
ImpressBooks.org
daveburgessconsulting.com

Library of Congress Control Number: 2021939756
Paperback ISBN: 978-1-948334-31-0
Ebook ISBN: 978-1-948334-32-7

Cover design by Emily Mahon
Interior design by Liz Schreiter
Editing and production by Reading List Editorial: readinglisteditorial.com

For all the teachers who spent their evenings and weekends adapting to the demands of the pandemic, this book is for you. I hope it provides a path forward that makes you feel more confident teaching and reaching *all* students.

—Catlin Tucker

This book is dedicated to all the educators who believe that all means all. Our calling is not to reach some students, or most students, but to design instruction that honors every learner and provides them with equal opportunities, access, expectations, and hope. Thank you for making this book a part of your journey.

—Katie Novak

Contents

Duck Boats and Flexible Learning Landscapes

If you've ever traveled to Boston, Massachusetts, you have likely seen one of the great tourist attractions of the city—the duck boats. Visitors from all over the world "flock" to Boston to immerse themselves in a historical tour of the city. The tour is unique because it takes place aboard a "Duck," a WWII–style amphibious vehicle that travels seamlessly from land to water and back again. The flexible nature of the duck boat allows it to navigate from the golden-domed State House to Boston Common past the cobblestoned streets of Quincy Market right into the Charles River.

Education today requires the same flexibility and agility. We are called to design and deliver curriculum and instruction that engages learners in person, online, or via a blend of the two, and back again. We don't need two vehicles—or two different sets of skills—to meet the needs of learners in a flexible learning landscape. Instead, we need an adaptable skill set that's flexible enough to travel from the bumpy cobblestone streets of traditional education to the choppy waters of online learning.

Every student deserves the best opportunity to develop their skills and knowledge, whatever the learning landscape. For too long, schools were designed for mythical "average learners" at the expense of students who have unique needs and who challenge teachers to discover the limits of their commitments, insights, and skills.[1] Too many learners are not successful in our systems, and so change and innovation are necessary.

The National Assessment of Educational Progress (NAEP) is one measure by which the United States assesses student performance and achievement. We recognize the limitations of large-scale standardized assessments and the inherent inequities in the design of such assessments. These barriers aside, it is devastating that in 2019 (the most recent data available), achievement nationwide was lower than in 2017. In 2019, for example, 34 percent of eighth-grade students performed at or above proficient in reading compared to 37 percent in 2017. In math, 34 percent of eighth graders were proficient in math compared to 35 percent in 2017. When examining the achievement gap more closely, we see the largest gaps exist for historically marginalized groups, including students with disabilities, English language learners, students from low-income families, and underrepresented minority students—traditionally defined as African American, Hispanic, and Indigenous students.[2]

Additionally, student engagement is increasingly problematic. According to research, 66 percent of surveyed students reported being bored in every class or at least every day in school. Of these students, 98 percent claimed the material being taught was the main reason for their boredom, 81 percent thought their subject material was uninteresting, and two out of three students found the material lacked relevance.[3]

What is heartbreaking about the results is that teachers and students are working way too hard to not have better outcomes. We believe, without a doubt, teachers and administrators are doing everything they can to increase student achievement, engagement, and autonomy. It is just that many of our practices are not flexible enough, or adaptable enough, to meet the needs of a diverse student population in a changing educational landscape.

Despite the effort, intent, and successes we experience in education today, as educators, we have to recognize that we continue to live and teach in a climate of inequity. Many practices, policies, and procedures in our schools and districts create disproportionate outcomes for students.

In the spring of 2020, COVID-19 disrupted education on a large scale. With mandatory stay-at-home orders, millions of educators and learners shifted to remote teaching and learning. Terms like *remote learning*, *at-home learning*, and *distance learning* became the norm. What had the potential to be flexible and responsive became "one-size-fits-all" learning online, with students required to spend hours on screen, following the same pathways at the same pace. The affordances and potential benefits of learning online were ignored.

To be clear, this is not a book about COVID-19 or remote learning. Enough books have been written about distance learning and remote learning. We want to offer something more comprehensive. Teaching and learning landscapes are not dichotomous. It's not in-person learning *or* online learning, as if learning is relegated to one mode at a time. Teaching and learning today is not as simple as this or that but requires the flexibility to navigate multiple learning landscapes simultaneously. Whether learning is in-person, online, or involves a combination of the two, students need high expectations, flexible pathways, and autonomy to become expert learners.

Simon Sinek, a leadership expert, popularized the phrase "Start with why."[4] He argues everyone has a *why*. It's what inspires us. Too often, our students aren't inspired in school because we don't ground our lessons and assessments in their *why*. Instead, we focus on *what* and *where*. We focus on standards, curriculum, standardized assessments, and the method of delivery. But that's not *why* they learn.

The purpose of teaching, regardless of the learning landscape, is to inspire students to learn and to cultivate lifelong learners.

The *what* and *where* are only the beginning. It's too easy to google *what*, to recall *what*, to regurgitate *what*. Our students don't need to know only that they will read *The Merchant of Venice*, complete a step-by-step lab on photosynthesis, solve quadratic equations, or write an argument paper on the causes of World War II. They also have to know *why* it's a privilege to read critically, solve problems, and communicate clearly, and how those skills can help them to change our world.

We can't focus too much on *where* learning is happening— whether it's in person, online, or via an ever-changing combination of the two. Instead, we need a skill set that's flexible enough to start with the *why*. To do this, we need to provide our students with options and choices to personalize their learning paths. We need to help students understand their purpose and *why* the art of learning deserves their attention. If you can't find a *why*, then the *what* and the *where* will fall short.

To meet the needs of diverse learners in flexible landscapes, educators need more than a single framework. Universal Design for Learning (UDL) reminds us the goal of school is to teach students how to become motivated, resourceful, innovative learners and to help them prepare for the lives they want to live. To do this, we have to embrace blended learning so our pedagogical practices can seamlessly traverse from in-person, hybrid, online, and back again. Just like the duck boats.

Connecting UDL and Blended Learning

Together, we want to help educators navigate an ever-changing learning landscape with confidence and ease. To do this, we want to make the connection between UDL and blended learning clear.

Throughout the book, we will each share our expertise with the corresponding frameworks and make explicit connections between the frameworks and your practice. Our *why* is to help you, as readers, recognize the power and promise of implementing UDL in a blended learning environment. Before we help you figure out your *why*, we want to share how we came to this shared space.

Why UDL and Blended Learning?

Katie

I was always destined to be a teacher. As the daughter of two teachers, I grew up in a small town in the suburbs of Providence, Rhode Island, just over the border in Massachusetts. My siblings and I still lovingly refer to Seekonk as "The Konk." My mom was a fifth-grade teacher at North Elementary School, so like many teacher's kids, I was programmed to be compliant lest I hear "Do you want me to call Kathy?" My dad was a college instructor in video production. As a child, I saw the long hours they spent planning and understood the weight of the students they cared about and loved. On one occasion, my mom spent hours baking brownies and chopping Oreos and Nilla Wafers so students could better understand the layers of the earth. My parents both worked late into the night, and work spilled into the weekends as they designed projects, assessed student work, and spent hours on the phone with colleagues, triaging for students they served.

I went to college with the goal of being a doctor or a therapist, someone with more defined hours, I thought, but never felt like I found my way. After graduating with a degree in Recreational Therapy, I spent what they now call a "gap year" trying to figure out what I wanted to do. I taught dance classes to preschool students, waited tables, and tended bar, fine-tuning the art of the perfect pour.

When I returned to school to earn a master's degree in teaching, I fell into the same rhythm my parents had: connecting with students and families, designing lessons and assessments, analyzing student work, and repeating. My career in education had a rough start. I was nonrenewed after my first year of teaching. This nonrenewal, after I got over the initial sting, lit a fire in me. I wanted to prove to myself and prove to my administrators, who didn't see a future for me in education, that I was capable. No, better than capable.

I taught high school and middle school English for twelve years before transitioning to administration and then consulting, but I don't think of my career pivoting when I became an administrator. The biggest shift in my career was when I learned about Universal Design for Learning (UDL).

As a seventh-grade English teacher, my district was selected to be a part of a research project on district implementation of UDL, working directly with CAST, the organization that created the framework. District leadership encouraged me to join an early adoption cohort. My answer was a hard no. The previous year, I had earned my doctorate, piloted coteaching, facilitated consultancy protocols, advised the newspaper club, and coached cross-country. I was burnt out, very pregnant, and not interested in taking one for the team. Luckily, the assistant superintendent at the time, Dr. Kristan Rodriguez, who is a brilliant woman and a dear friend, refused to take no for an answer.

"This opportunity was made for you," she said, over and over again. Eventually, I relented. I would attend the week-long institute in the summer, but I wouldn't commit to anything long-term. And then, I learned about UDL and saw an opportunity to transform my planning, my classroom, and my learners' outcomes. I was hooked.

Before I learned about UDL, I was dealing out tattered paperbacks of the classics like it was my life's calling. The whole class read *The Outsiders* and then the whole class read *The Old Man and the*

Sea. I excitedly circulated the books, week after week, to groaning middle schoolers slumped in their chairs. After I assigned reading, I gave a multiple-choice test or a pop quiz, and some students got As and others did not. Good grades were bestowed upon those students who were either a) proficient readers or b) creative enough to come up with another strategy, like watching the movie, reading Sparknotes, or asking their friends what the chapter was about. There were always a handful of students who admittedly did not read a single page of the book and told me, "These books are torture. How are they relevant to me at all? Who cares about this?" Touché.

In my ongoing work with CAST that year, I learned about the importance of firm goals and flexible means, the power of student voice, and how to design learning experiences to help students become expert learners. By slowing down and asking students what they needed, by co-creating flexible options and choices for how to learn and share what they know, and by carving out one day a week we coined as "Hooray, Hooray, It's Rewrite Day" for revisions, review, and small-group instruction, student learning significantly increased.

My plan was to stay in the classroom, just like my mom, but Kristan Rodriguez had other ideas. She encouraged me to apply to be the district reading coordinator. Again, the first time it was a hard no. "But think about the impact you can make by supporting your colleagues!" she said. And so I served as a district coordinator of reading and a Title 1 director, and then an assistant superintendent of schools, always seeing myself as a teacher at heart.

I designed faculty meeting structures, professional learning communities, and professional development sessions using the same core beliefs and principles I modeled with students. And as technology has evolved and become more flexible and more advanced, I design flexible learning experiences that occur online, offline, and back again. It is flexible, like the duck boats, and honors our students as learners.

Me, a Teacher?

Catlin

If you had told me in high school I was going to be a teacher, I would have laughed you out of the room. *Who in their right mind would want to be a teacher?* Despite being a diligent and hardworking student, I wasn't particularly inspired by my teachers, my classes, or school. I remember only a handful of my teachers' names and received the type of education that was common for people of my generation. I understood my job was to sit quietly, take copious notes, and complete my assignments. I don't remember vibrant class discussions or engaging collaborative projects. I remember sitting at hard desks, arranged in rows, listening to endless lectures.

Given my uninspired experiences as a student, you may be wondering how I wandered into this profession. A trip I took to Ireland with my best friend, Sara, was the first domino to fall in a chain of happy accidents that led me to a career in education. I was a junior at the University of California in Los Angeles majoring in English literature when Sara announced one night at dinner that she was going to spend five months abroad. At the time, I was on track to follow in my mother's footsteps and pursue a career in law. I was even going to graduate early because I had taken classes during the summer quarters. But when I heard about Sara's trip, I decided to change my plans.

Instead of graduating early, I took the summer before my senior year and the fall quarter off and joined Sara for a trip that would change the trajectory of my life. Sara and I landed in Cork, Ireland, in the summer of 1999 and managed to get a job on St. Patrick Street at Gloria Jean's coffee shop where we worked the till (cash register), made coffee and tea, and assembled baps (sandwiches). On our days off, we hopped on trains to travel around Ireland and Europe. At the end of our four months in Cork, we took the money we had saved from our job at the coffee shop and planned a five-week backpacking adventure around Europe.

During our trip, I began to question my decision to be a lawyer. Did I want to spend my days working in an office? I had watched my mom work tirelessly for years, often seven days a week. No, I didn't want to go to law school. But what was I going to do with my English degree? Could I be an English teacher? I thought about the hours of a school day and the summers off. A career as a teacher would afford me time to travel and write, two things I discovered I was passionate about.

In a hostel in Amsterdam, I filled out an application for the teaching credential program at the University of California at Santa Barbara, barely making the filing deadline. When I returned to the States, I received a letter with a date and time for my interview. I was accepted into the program and told my parents about my change of heart and my change in plans. They were stunned. "Are you sure you want to be a teacher?" It was clear my family had some serious concerns about whether I was well-suited for a career in education.

While in my credential and master's program at UCSB, I fantasized about my future classroom. I imagined my students bounding through the door, eager and excited to learn. I pictured them sitting in circles talking animatedly about literature and life. The reality of my first few years in this profession stood in stark contrast to these elaborate fantasies. Instead of bounding through the door, my students trudged. They refused to engage in conversation or take risks. It was jarring.

I quickly became exhausted and disillusioned with the profession. These feelings stemmed from the realization that I was failing.

I was failing to create the classroom I had dreamed about. I was failing to engage my students in dynamic learning experiences. I was failing to inspire my students in the same way my teachers had failed me. Had I made an enormous mistake becoming a teacher? It was at this moment of career crisis that I inadvertently stumbled onto technology.

My career crisis coincided with my decision to have my first child. While on maternity leave, I decided to teach college-level writing courses to supplement our income and provide me with a challenge and mental stimulation. I would not describe myself as technology savvy, or even that interested in technology, prior to this experience, but my work as an online professor piqued my interest in the power of technology. I was particularly intrigued by my students' interactions in our online discussion forum. Even though they needed support navigating this online communication space, I saw them grow and develop the skills necessary to engage with each other in meaningful dialogue.

When I returned to my high school classroom after a year at home with my daughter, I was determined to give the teaching profession one more year. I decided to treat my classroom like a laboratory and experiment with the online learning strategies I'd become familiar with teaching my online college classes. It was 2008, and my public high school was low-tech. I had to leverage the devices that walked through the door in my students' pockets. Almost everything my students did with the technology required conversation and collaboration as they shared devices. I realize now this early approach to using technology to foster collaboration has informed much of my work on blended learning.

The results of my experimentation were nothing short of magical. I began to reimagine my role in the learning process and slowly shifted the focus away from myself in the design and facilitation of our lessons. I didn't need to have all of the answers or supply all of the information. Instead, I challenged students to ask and answer their own questions, to investigate, explore, and make meaning, and work together to create artifacts of their learning they were proud of. A few months into this experimentation, I had created the classroom I had dreamed about in credential school. Students were engaged in conversations, leaning into the learning, and taking risks.

It was that early blend of online and offline learning that changed my reality as a teacher and ignited my passion for this profession. I learned many powerful lessons from my work blending offline and online learning. It forced me to reevaluate my value. Instead of feeling the pressure to be the expert of everything, I began to let go and allow my students to develop their own expertise. I spent less time at the front of the room transferring information and telling students everything I knew about a topic or a text. I spent more time working with small groups of learners or individual students to effectively support them as they developed their content knowledge and honed skills. I realized my value did not lie in my subject-area expertise but rather in my ability to connect with learners. I embraced my role as a coach and facilitator and designed learning experiences that allowed me to spend more time on the human side of this work, which is critical to learning.

In the last ten years, I've written five books on blended learning. I have worked as a blended learning coach, supporting teachers in shifting their mindsets, skill sets, and toolsets to leverage blended learning models to transfer control over the learning experience to students. In 2017, I began my doctoral program in learning technologies at Pepperdine University. I researched teacher engagement in blended learning environments and successfully defended my dissertation in July 2020. The timing could not have been better. That summer, schools all over the country were in crisis, trying to prepare for an uncertain 2020–2021 school year. My experience in the fields of blended and online learning helped me support teachers in this transition to online and blended learning environments. As I work with schools and teachers, I want to help them reimagine teaching and learning to shift students to the center of learning.

Know Better, Do Better

We wrote this book to help educators develop confidence in their ability to traverse any learning terrain. To shift from surviving to thriving. To paraphrase Maya Angelou, when we know better, we do better. Most educational institutions were not prepared for the sudden shift online necessitated by the pandemic. This quick transition left leaders, teachers, students, and families scrambling. It was hard for us to listen to media outlets slam educators for a rocky transition to online learning when teachers were doing their best with the tools and training they had available. Few were trained—pedagogically or technologically—for the demands of this shift.

Yet, we believe it is a mistake to think this pandemic is the last time we are likely to see education interrupted. As Justin Reich, executive director of the MIT Teaching Systems Lab and co-founder of EdTechTeacher, said in an article published by *Mindshift*, "There are going to be more pandemics and there are going to be more disruptions because of climate change. We do have to get better as a society at building interrupted school systems."[5] We agree. There are likely to be more interruptions and disruptions, but it is our hope educators will feel more prepared to navigate those situations and use a blend of online and offline learning to engage all students regardless of the learning landscape.

Instead of dismissing online learning as a failure because it was hard or we (and our students) felt unprepared for it, we need to cultivate the skills necessary to weave together the best aspects of face-to-face learning and online learning using the principles of Universal Design. We must develop a skill set that's nimble enough to help us transition from one learning landscape to the other without disruption. We must use this moment as a catalyst for positive changes that will include:

- A shift from breadth to depth and from minutiae to meaning.
- A recognition that relationships and connection matter more than curriculum and standardized tests.
- An understanding that all students learn in their own unique ways and a one-size-fits-all approach fails the majority of students.

Let's seize this moment as an opportunity to reimagine learning to better serve *all* students. We hope this book helps you to emerge from this challenging moment stronger, more flexible, and more confident.

SUMMARIZE, REFLECT, AND DISCUSS

- Simon Sinek, a leadership expert, argues that everyone has a *why*. When you think about your work in education, what is your *why*?
- This book is focused on meeting the needs of all learners through Universal Design for Learning (UDL) and blended learning. Consider what you know about each of the frameworks and make connections to your practice. It may be helpful to brainstorm a definition for each, or share your thoughts in a blog or on social media, so you can see how your understanding deepens as you read.
- COVID-19 launched us into a flexible learning landscape that will continue to evolve. What are some best practices you have implemented in a flexible learning landscape? What are your biggest challenges or questions about teaching and learning in flexible learning landscapes?

CHAPTER 1

Wuzzles, Universal Design, and Blended Learning

The Potential of Mixing It Up

Katie

Saturday morning cartoons were all the rage in the 1980s. Every Saturday morning, I wheeled the piano bench from the den so I could set up a makeshift TV tray for my Cream of Wheat and mug of hot cocoa. Watching television was a rare treat. We weren't allowed to watch during the week, so on Saturday morning, I sat, mesmerized by animated friends. Leaning over the bench, syrup dripping from my chin, I took in the lineup of *Muppet Babies*, *The Smurfs*, and *Alvin and the Chipmunks*. A lesser-known classic, *The Wuzzles*, was my favorite.

The Wuzzles was a fanciful cartoon about creatures who were two different animals combined. According to the show, the word *wuzzle* meant "to mix up." For my birthday, I asked for a plush version of Bumblelion, who was half bumblebee and half lion. The same year, I was Hoppopotamus—half rabbit, half hippopotamus—for Halloween.

There was something so incredibly whimsical about the Wuzzles and how two different animals could merge together. Each animal had important characteristics, but together, they were . . . better. I mean, a lion who is courageous *and* can fly? Kismet.

Universal Design for Learning (UDL) and blended learning (BL) can create a more inclusive, more equitable, more innovative learning landscape that meets the needs of all our learners. But before diving into how UDL and BL work together, let's unpack the core components and characteristics of the UDL framework.

What Is Universal Design for Learning?

UDL grew out of efforts to help students who were underserved in schools, especially those with disabilities. The innovation came in realizing that lowering barriers for those students also lowered previously unseen barriers for learners who were not identified for special education. This in turn led to a recognition that universally designed education would encompass all learners because human variability is a continuum of difference that changes according to context, opportunity, etc.

The term *Universal Design* was coined by architect Ronald Mace in 1988. He defined it as the "design of products and environments to be usable by all people, to the greatest extent possible, without the need for adaptation or specialized design."[1] Buildings that not all people could enter were deemed "architecturally disabling." UDL adapts Mace's definition to learning.

When working with educators and schools all over the world, we are sometimes met with "Oh, UDL? We're already doing that." The truth is, we are often not. The practice of providing choice in a classroom is often mistaken for UDL, and while choice is certainly a component of UDL, it hardly defines it. If we were truly implementing UDL, all students would have access to advanced coursework, all students would be making progress toward grade-level standards, all students would have autonomy and agency over their learning, and we wouldn't be making so many damn copies at the copy machine.

We need authentic, self-differentiated, flexible learning to provide equal opportunities for our learners to succeed, regardless of the learning landscape. Our schools are not working equally for all students because we often rely on one-size-fits-all practices out of habit, we don't know what else to do, or we don't believe all kids are capable of deep learning in inclusive classrooms. Moving toward full and genuine implementation of UDL is critical.

Oftentimes, educators hear about UDL and think of it as a checklist or collection of strategies. UDL isn't something you do as much as something you believe about teaching and learning. The UDL framework recognizes and embraces learner variability and provides a lens for creating instructional goals, methods, materials, and assessments that work for everyone—not a single, one-size-fits-all solution. The "universal" concept means we can design a lesson with enough flexibility to work for all learners that remains focused on the same firm goals.

David Rose is a cofounder of CAST and a father of UDL. In a book he coauthored, *Universal Design for Learning: Theory and Practice,* he wrote, "Most curricula are designed and developed as if students were homogeneous, and the most common approach to curriculum design is to address the needs of the so-called 'average student.' Of course, this average student is a myth, a statistical artifact not corresponding to any actual individual. But because so much of the curriculum and teaching methods employed in most schools are based on the needs of this mythical average student, they are also laden with inadvertent and unnecessary barriers to learning."[2]

The Higher Education Opportunity Act defines UDL as "a scientifically valid framework for guiding educational practice that (a) provides flexibility in the ways information is presented, in the ways students respond or demonstrate knowledge and skills, and in the ways students are engaged; and (b) reduces barriers in instruction, provides appropriate accommodations, supports, and challenges, and maintains high achievement expectations for all students, including students with disabilities."[3]

If we want all students to have equal opportunities to learn, we have to be incredibly purposeful, proactive, and flexible. This work begins with beliefs about students and the power of design and flexibility to eliminate barriers to learning.

A UDL practitioner believes:

- Variability is the rule, not the exception. Students may need to learn in different ways, using different materials, at different paces, to reach the same goals.
- All students can work toward the same firm goals and grade-level standards when provided with nurturing conditions and adequate support.
- All students will become expert learners if barriers are removed.

These beliefs are the seeds of UDL. All the UDL strategies in the world won't transform practice if they aren't in service of the belief that all students can learn, regardless of variability. And to provide equal opportunities to learn, we have to be incredibly flexible, commit to iterative design, and ensure we can elevate and celebrate deep learning regardless of the learning landscape.

Streaming Digital TV and Designing for Autonomy

Do you remember what watching television used to be like before streaming? Programming was on a set schedule. If we wanted to watch *Friends* growing up, we had to be home and parked on the couch every Thursday night at 8:00 p.m. We had to wait for a commercial break to use the bathroom. And the season finale always left us frustrated, as we'd have to wait an entire summer before learning whether or not Ross and Rachel were getting together. It was torture. We had zero control over our experience as viewers.

Our children have no idea what pre-streaming television was like. They decide what they watch, when they watch, where they watch, and how much they watch (with parent approval, of course). They can pause an episode at any moment to grab a snack or use the bathroom. They rewind an episode if we dare to interrupt and intrude on their experience.

Streaming has shifted control from the networks to the viewer. Our children personalize the experience every time they select content. They control the pace of their progress through a show and decide how much time they will spend watching a particular show . . . one episode or three?

The traditional approach to teaching shares several similarities with network television. Students, like viewers, have to be in a particular place at a particular time to learn and have little to no control over the content or substance of their learning.

It should not surprise anyone that a network television approach to education fails to engage the majority of learners. You might get lucky channel surfing and stumble upon a rerun of a favorite show or an iconic movie like *The Breakfast Club*. There is a momentary thrill when you think, "Score! *The Breakfast Club!*" It is quickly followed by the realization you'll have to sit through endless commercials, but you may stick with it if there isn't anything better on.

We equate these TV treasures with those teachers who light up a room and captivate students' attention. We've all had teachers who somehow pull us in with their personalities, energy, and passion for their subjects, even if we are not particularly interested in geometry or world history. But although these teachers may captivate the students lucky enough to land in their classrooms, the ability to control one's learning experience is more likely to move the masses in terms of engagement and motivation.

Like streaming, blended learning is designed to give students control over the time, place, pace, and path of their learning experience. Yet this intentional transfer of control from teacher to learner is often absent from the conversation. It's because giving up control is scary. It requires us to trust students and believe they are capable of driving their learning.

What Is Blended Learning?

Blended learning is the combination of active, engaged learning online combined with active, engaged learning offline to provide students with more control over the time, place, pace, and path of their learning. This definition is adapted from Staker and Horn's oft-cited definition, and it reflects a constructivist perspective, placing emphasis on the student's role as an active participant in the learning process.[4]

TIME AND PLACE. Blended learning acknowledges learning is not restricted to a particular time or place. Though "seat time" requirements suggest a physical body needs to be in a particular location at a particular time to learn, students benefit when they move around, make observations, experiment and tinker, and engage with people beyond the classroom.

It's incredible to consider that we live in a time when we can access information and learn from just about anywhere, anytime. We can log on to the internet thirty thousand feet in the air and work while traveling or record a quick voice memo to capture an idea for a blog post while on a hike. That flexibility and ease of access should be reflected in our formal educational system.

PACE. Blended learning values the student's ability to control the pace of learning. Pacing can make or break an experience. If a lesson moves too quickly, some students fall behind, become frustrated, and disengage. If a lesson moves too slowly, some students get bored, become frustrated, and disengage. See the pattern? It is impossible to maximize engagement when learners are asked to move lockstep through learning experiences. So why do we continue to use this approach in classrooms all over the world while simultaneously lamenting a lack of student engagement? If we want to maximize engagement, we have to design learning experiences that allow students more control over the pace.

PATH. Blended learning acknowledges the path each learner takes to get from point A to point B may need to be different. Some learners will take a direct route without needing any assistance. Others will need road signs and a map or an alternate route to make the journey. Still others will benefit from following an experienced guide who has an intimate understanding of the terrain.

To personalize a learner's path, we must understand what our learners need and make time to connect with them throughout the learning process to ensure those needs are being met. Teachers must lean on instructional models that create the time and space for these critical conversations about progress and path.

Too often, schools invest in technology, improve the wireless infrastructure, purchase a learning management system (LMS), and call it blended learning. There is a distinct difference between a technology-rich learning environment and a student-centered blended learning environment. If we are not pairing that technology, Wi-Fi, and LMS with a shift in the way we design and facilitate learning, we will not be successful in shifting the focus and control from teachers to learners.

Failed Date Night Needs a Blended Learning Makeover

Catlin

To understand this distinction between a technology-rich learning environment and blended learning, let me tell you the story of a failed date night. Several years ago, my husband and I were invited to join another couple for an evening out at a culinary school in wine country that opens its doors on the weekend. Couples can spend an evening cooking in a state-of-the-art kitchen under the guidance of a trained chef.

As I entered the kitchen where we would spend the first ninety minutes of our evening cooking, I took in the space. It was vast and sharply contrasted with my modest kitchen at home. Each couple was assigned a workstation. There were stainless steel work tables, giant chopping boards, a collection of knives and other cooking utensils (many of which were foreign to me), industrial-size pots, pans in every size, and a grill that had ten burners! There were mixers, microwaves, and metal bowls nested like Russian dolls. Every possible cooking instrument was available to us for the evening.

"Let the cooking commence!" the chef announced. We were given a printed recipe and a collection of ingredients. "Tonight, you will prepare coq au vin with roasted red potatoes and sautéed string beans. For dessert, you will make a crème brûlée." The menu for the evening was set. Each couple was making the same dish.

Twenty minutes into our cooking lesson, I was looking at the clock, silently working out how much more time I would have to stay in this room listening to this chef and following directions as he guided us through the process of making our meal. I felt guilty. This was supposed to be a fun date night for me, my husband, and our friends, but I wasn't enjoying it.

The chef kept asking us to pause in our work to watch him explain or demonstrate something. I am not a culinary artist by any stretch of the imagination, but I cook every night for my family and have honed the skills necessary to be competent in a kitchen. I know how to hold a knife. I'm skilled at chopping and dicing. I understand how to grill, sauté, and fry. So each time the chef instructed us to stop so he could demonstrate a technique or explain something that I already knew how to do, I was annoyed. The experience had the jerky quality of starting and stopping, like being stuck in rush-hour traffic.

Not only did I not enjoy the constant interruptions, but I was preparing a meal I was not particularly excited about. I have been a vegetarian for most of my life, so I would not be feasting on the coq au vin when we transitioned to the dining room to eat. Instead, like so much of my experience as a vegetarian, I would get an extra helping of the vegetables. Don't get me wrong, I love vegetables, but it was hard to feel invested in braising a chicken that I wasn't going to eat.

Even though I had all the tools I could possibly need to thrive in the kitchen, the lack of autonomy and control soured the experience. I would have preferred making dinner at home. Cooking in a restaurant-style kitchen helped me to appreciate the simple pleasures associated with cooking a meal for my family. I enjoy finding my own recipes, moving at my own pace, sipping a glass of wine, and escaping mentally while moving around my scantily stocked kitchen to make dinner.

My experience that night is like a lot of students' experiences in a technology-rich classroom. They have all the devices and software they could possibly need to learn. They have an expert guiding the experience. However, if those tools and expertise are not paired with a student-centered approach to the design and facilitation of the learning experience, the lesson may fall flat.

Like my lack of enthusiasm for the dish I was creating, students with no control over what they are learning are unlikely to feel invested in the experience, even if they are lucky enough to work in a technology-rich environment.

Similar to my frustration with the chef, students may feel stifled working on a teacher's timeline. They may resent being stopped and asked to listen to an explanation or watch a model they don't need. They may also need more or less time than their peers to navigate a task. The more autonomy they have over their pace of progress, the more likely they are to stay engaged in the learning activity.

If our chef had begun our session by providing us with basic instruction and modeling specific techniques, then allowed each group of couples to work at their own pace, the night would have been exponentially more enjoyable. Instead of stationing himself at the demonstration table the entire evening, I wish he had circulated around the massive kitchen, connecting with and supporting the different couples as they cooked. The room was clearly composed of a range of competencies when it came to cooking, so addressing the entire group when one person was struggling with a step in the recipe seemed an inefficient way to approach the night. However, that's often what happens in a lot of classrooms. Instead of offering support, scaffolds, or reteaching to the handful of students who need it, teachers often stop the whole class and ask them to pause what they are doing and listen.

Like that state-of-the-art kitchen, a classroom full of technology will not transform learning. Transformation requires a shift in mindset or the values and beliefs that drive a teacher's work. However, it is easier to spend money on technology than change mindsets.

A Blended Learning Mindset

The Aurora Institute, previously called the International Association for K-12 Online Learning (iNACOL), published a framework of blended learning teacher competencies in which they identify the importance of mindset as a cornerstone of transformation in education. A blended learning teacher must embrace a "new vision for teaching and learning" and possess an "orientation toward change and improvement."[5]

A NEW VISION FOR TEACHING AND LEARNING. The blended learning teacher must value a student-centered approach to learning, collaborate with stakeholders, create flexible learning environments, strive to personalize learning, demonstrate a desire to continue learning and growing, and be creative and driven.

Shifting a teacher's mindset is challenging. Our assumptions about what it means to be teachers and learners are ingrained in us from a young age. Teachers draw both consciously and unconsciously from their own experiences as students in classrooms to guide their work. Yet our world has changed dramatically in the last twenty years. Technology has permeated every aspect of our society.

Our students have grown up with devices in their hands. They can communicate anytime from anywhere. They can document every aspect of their lives and share that documentation online. They can stream and binge media. When they want to learn at home, they watch a YouTube video. Given these dramatic shifts in the way people access, consume, process, and share information, it makes sense that everyone involved in education takes a step back and reevaluates what we are doing and *why* we are doing it.

At the core of this new vision for teaching and learning is a realization that the learner *must* have some control over the learning experience for learning to be relevant, engaging, and meaningful. Without control, learners are passive consumers watching mindless television they do not care about.

ORIENTATION TOWARD CHANGE AND IMPROVEMENT. The blended learning teacher must also embrace uncertainty, model growth and change, respond to individual student needs, and cultivate independent, self-directed learners capable of driving the learning.

This orientation toward change necessitates that the teacher be the lead learner in a classroom. Instead of believing our value is wrapped up in our expertise, be that subject-area or pedagogical expertise, teachers must appreciate that their true value lies in their ability to connect with learners—the human side of teaching. Those teachers who understand this truth are not scared of technology or threatened by new approaches to teaching and learning. They understand that the value they bring to a learning environment cannot be replaced by technology.

The shift from expert to facilitator is a critical mindset shift. It requires less preparation and planning to stand in front of a group of students and tell them everything we know about a topic, issue, or text. It is much more cognitively challenging to design, or "architect," learning experiences that invite students to wrestle with complex concepts to make their own meaning. As students engage with the learning experience and each other, our job is to facilitate, coach, and guide. Facilitation demands flexibility, human connection, and a toolbox of strategies the teacher can draw from to support a wide range of learners. When teachers successfully facilitate learning, they allow students to experience the thrill of discovery, the lightbulb, the ah-ha moment that makes learning so exciting and rewarding.

Blended Learning Models

Blended learning is an umbrella term. Within the umbrella are many different models teachers can use to blend online and offline learning. On one end of the blended learning spectrum are the rotation models, like the station rotation and flipped classroom models, that rely on the teacher as the primary driver of instruction and in which learning happens primarily in a classroom. On the other end of the spectrum are models that rely on online instruction as the primary driver of learning, and in which the majority of learning happens online with periodic face-to-face check-ins with the teacher of record.[6]

The various models give students different degrees of control over time, place, pace, and path. Students are unlikely to control all of these aspects of their learning at one time, but the goal is to give them *more* control more of the time.

Most schools focus on the rotation models because they work beautifully in a traditional school setting. They are also flexible enough to transcend a specific learning landscape. As the pandemic has made clear, flexibility is key.

Let's review the rotation models since they will be mentioned throughout this text.

THE WHOLE GROUP ROTATION MODEL. This is an updated version of the lab-rotation model, which was included in the original taxonomy of blended learning models.[7] The whole group rotation moves the class as a unit between online and offline learning activities, freeing the teacher to work one-on-one with learners during the online portions of the lesson, as pictured in figure 1.1.[8] As a result, this model necessitates that all learners have access to a device for the online learning portions of the lesson.

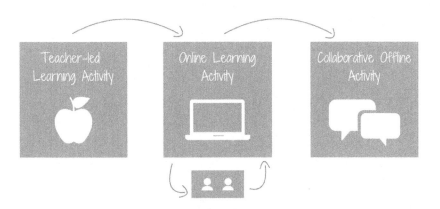

Figure 1.1: The Whole Group Rotation

During the online learning portions of the lesson, the goal is to differentiate or personalize the learning experience and free the teacher to support individual students by providing one-on-one coaching. By contrast, the offline time may be teacher-led or used to encourage communication and collaboration among the members of the learning community.

Benefits of the whole group rotation include students having increased access to personalized instruction and practice during the online learning tasks, more control over the pace of their progress through the online portion of the lesson, and opportunities to work directly with the teacher and with peers to improve the quality of the learning.

THE STATION ROTATION MODEL. The station rotation model is composed of a series of stations, or learning activities, that students rotate through. Unlike the whole group rotation, teachers with limited devices in the classroom can utilize this model as it does not require all students to be online simultaneously.

Typically, a station rotation lesson includes a teacher-led station, an online station, and an offline station, as pictured in figure 1.2. However, the total number of stations may vary depending on several different factors, such as the length of a class period and the number of students in a class. Similarly, a station rotation can span a single class period or extend over multiple periods.

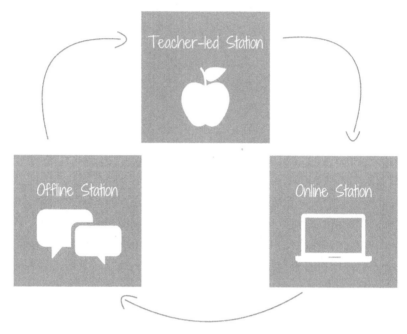

Figure 1.2: The Basic Design of a Station Rotation Lesson

The benefits of the station rotation model include the ability to create smaller learning communities within a large class; work directly with small groups of learners; provide more control over the pace of learning at the online and offline stations; and create more opportunities to differentiate learning experiences, group students strategically, and foster communication and collaboration among learners.

If teachers think of stations as learning activities instead of physical locations in a classroom and a rotation as a shift from one learning activity to the next instead of physical movement in a classroom, it is easier to appreciate the flexibility of this model.

THE FLIPPED CLASSROOM MODEL. The flipped classroom model inverts the traditional approach to instruction and application, as shown in figure 1.3. The transfer of information (mini-lessons, lectures, and explanations) is captured using media, usually video, so that students can self-pace through that content pausing, rewinding, and rewatching as needed. This "flipped" instruction can be viewed at home or during asynchronous work time. Then, synchronous class time can be used to prioritize practice and application. That way, students have access to the subject-area expert and their peers for support as they work. The teacher can pull individual students for additional instruction, support, or guided practice.

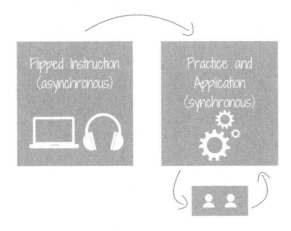

Figure 1.3: The Flipped Classroom Model

The primary benefit of the flipped classroom is the students' ability to control the pace at which they consume and process information. As teachers create video content, they build a repository of resources that learners can access on-demand anytime, anywhere. The flipped classroom model also provides higher levels of teacher and peer support as students attempt to apply what they are learning.

THE PLAYLIST MODEL. The playlist model is a twist on the individual rotation model. Students self-pace through a playlist of learning activities that mixes media, learning modalities, and online with offline tasks, as illustrated in figure 1.4.

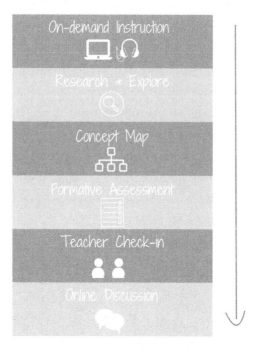

Figure 1.4: The Playlist Model

The path of a playlist can be differentiated to meet the needs of groups of learners with different skill levels, interests, or language proficiencies. Teachers can also personalize the path by building in "teacher check-ins," or periodic conferences, to review each student's individual progress. During these conferencing sessions, the teacher and the learner can decide what needs to be added to or modified on the playlist for the student to continue making progress. These conversations make personalizing the path of the playlist sustainable. Instead of feeling pressure to know what every student will need at the start of a playlist, the teacher check-ins create space to discuss each student's progress and adjust the playlist as needed.

These rotation models provide clear structures that educators can lean on as they blend online and offline learning to provide students more control over their experience. They serve as helpful guides as we reimagine teaching and learning.

The Benefits of UDL and Blended Learning

The shift in mindset and skill set required by UDL and blended learning demands time, energy, and effort. Yet time and energy are not resources most teachers have in abundance. If we are going to ask overworked teachers to embrace new instructional models, we have to be clear about what they can expect in return. How will this shift positively impact their lives? Why is it worth their time? What is the value proposition?

We'd argue the biggest benefit of implementing UDL and blended learning is the positive impact on student engagement. When we reflect on our goals for student learning, we often include some form of the word *engage* in our answers: engaging, engagement, engaged.

It is important to emphasize that universally designed blended learning positively impacts engagement because teachers have more opportunities to:

- remove barriers
- differentiate and personalize learning
- give students agency over their learning
- work directly with learners to support their individual progress
- mix learning modalities and media to improve learning outcomes
- foster communication and collaboration among members of the class
- invite learners to demonstrate and share their learning in a variety of ways

All of these shifts—personalization, agency, individualized support, access to a range of resources, and connection to a dynamic learning community—work in concert to positively impact student engagement in blended learning environments.

Teacher engagement and student engagement are inextricably linked. The reciprocal relationship between the levels of student engagement and teacher engagement suggest that improving student engagement will have a direct, positive impact on teacher engagement at work.[9] So that's the value proposition for teachers. If they invest the time and energy to shift practice and move from teacher-led whole group instruction to blended learning models, they're likely to find this work more mentally and emotionally rewarding.

Hitting the Slopes with UDL and Blended Learning

Imagine it's your birthday. You are hell-bent on getting everyone to participate in your idea of fun, so you plan a skiing party. The plan is to go early so you can be on the chairlift when the slopes open at 8:00 a.m. You fully expect to complete at least fifteen runs on black-diamond trails. Now, if you invite only expert skiers, you probably won't face too many barriers. The problem comes when you invite all of your friends, not just those friends who are expert skiers. If you invited us, for example, and brought us up to the top of that mountain, you better offer a scaffold that includes the ski patrol and a ski mobile. Although we have many strengths, black-diamond skiing is not one of them. And so giving us a choice of two black-diamond trails is not, in any way, universal.

In this scenario, our question for you is, "What's your goal?" It's to have an amazing, memorable birthday with your friends, right? If you plan a black-diamond ski trip, some of your friends will face barriers, and these barriers fall into two categories: access and engagement.

Individuals face barriers to access when they "can't do it" in that way. If you are committed to skiing, some of your friends may not know how to ski yet, so the black-diamond trail is inaccessible. Maybe you have a friend who just had ACL surgery. She simply cannot ski.

Some of your friends do know how to ski. Maybe one of them took lessons as a child—but the thing is, he hates it. He hates being cold; he hates the crowds; he hates all of the aches and pains that follow, and he doesn't want to do it. That's not an access barrier but an engagement barrier.

The way to eliminate barriers is to focus on the goal and provide options for meeting it in flexible ways. Your goal really isn't to force all your friends to ski. Your goal is to have an amazing birthday. You can rent a house in Aspen, Colorado, and share your plan is to ski all day in the mountains. You can let your friends know they can ski with you, take lessons, go snowboarding, or hang out in the ski lodge while reading books and having a cocktail. Let your friends know there will be a buffet dinner at 7:00 p.m., but before then, if skiing isn't their thing, they could head to the spa, visit antique shops, or take a much-needed rest at the house. You will still have a memorable birthday, but everyone can help you meet that goal in accessible and engaging ways.

Variability, the Three UDL Principles, and Blended Learning

Just like the historic duck boats in Boston, implementing UDL using blended learning models requires incredible flexibility. As educators, whether we teach PK-12, work in higher education, or support adults through professional learning, we simply can't rely on one-size-fits-all practices. Cognitive neuroscience has shown us there really is not an average student anywhere, so there is not a single practice, pathway, place, or pace that will equally meet the needs of our students, our teachers, or our world. If we are going to engage the learners we serve in inclusive and equitable classrooms, we have to be committed to ongoing change and thinking differently. One belief we need to kick to the curb is our overreliance on labels and their relationship to student learning.

There's a quote that's often attributed to Mark Twain: "All generalizations are false, including this one." As educators, we would be wise to heed that advice. Too often, we make decisions in our classrooms and our schools based on generalizations, or labels, that define what students are capable of as opposed to embracing student variability and flexible grouping.

In team meetings and over lunch, educators sometimes share their struggles with supporting students who have autism, ADHD, or are learning disabled. UDL rejects these labels as predictors of what students need or can do, as none of them can paint a picture of what an individual is capable of. For example, many educators will ask, "What does UDL look like for learners with ADHD or for English learners?" as if students within these groups are all the same.

All students have a unique mix of strengths and weaknesses, and we could use a hundred labels to describe each of them: loyal, ethical, responsible, dyslexic, kind, athletic. Also, many of these labels are incredibly contextual. You could say a student is strong at visual decoding until you catch her without her contacts in or when she has a migraine. Suddenly, being able to decode in a traditional sense doesn't apply. At that moment, the option to listen to an audiobook would work like a charm. In UDL, we don't make judgments about our learners based on labels but have high expectations and believe all of them are capable of success when we provide pathways and empower them to determine what they need at any given point in time.

Because our ability to learn is so contextual, we have to embrace predictable variability and allow learners to make decisions about the place, pace, and path they will take to learn, the materials they will use, and how they will share what they know. This is where the UDL principles come into play: they provide multiple means of engagement, multiple means of representation, and multiple means of action and expression.

PROVIDE MULTIPLE MEANS OF ENGAGEMENT: Engagement is at the core of every learning experience. If we want to empower our learners, we have to foster both attention and commitment by designing flexible, authentic, meaningful learning experiences.

On the surface, engagement is often thought of as students who are involved in the classroom and able to actively participate, but the research suggests engagement is far more complex. Engagement is equal parts attention and commitment.[10] Commitment requires the ability to sustain effort and persistence and the ability to self-regulate and cope with the rigor of academics and the classroom environment. Although some learners may face challenges in these areas, educators can design instruction to scaffold the development of these skills.

Teachers can leverage blended learning models to create the time and space for learners to develop their self-regulation skills by encouraging students to:

- set regular personal, academic, and/or behavior goals
- track and monitor their progress toward those goals
- discuss their goals and their progress in regular conferencing sessions with their teachers

Supporting learners in developing these skills, which we'll explore further in Chapter 6 when we discuss metacognition, is critical to thriving in a universally designed blended learning environment where teachers and students are partners in learning. If students see the connection between their actions and behaviors and their ability to achieve goals they care about, they are more likely to exhibit sustained effort and persistence in the face of academic challenges.

Students are also more likely to expend effort and remain tenacious in the face of challenges if they feel they are part of a dynamic learning community. Teachers can create a support network for students if they design lessons that encourage communication and collaboration. For example, teachers using the station rotation model can effectively shift the focus from the teacher to the learners so that groups of students must negotiate tasks together. In fact, the beauty of all blended learning models is the shift from teacher-centered to student-centered learning environments, which is critical to increasing student engagement.

As teachers shift from one-size-fits-all lessons to universally designed blended learning experiences, they can give students more agency. The way in which we architect lessons should acknowledge learner variability in terms of their interests. It is impossible for teachers to know what lights every student up, or what they are passionate about, which is why getting to know students and building agency and choice into the learning is key for keeping students engaged. As we design lessons, universally designed blended learning prioritizes agency and invites students to make key decisions about their learning.

- What does the student want to learn? What aspect of the larger topic are they interested in? What lens do they want to look through?
- How do they want to get from point A to point B? What path do they want to take? What materials or tools do they want to use? Would they like to work online or offline?
- What would they like to create to demonstrate their learning? How can they feel successful communicating or sharing what they know or learned?

The more decisions our students get to make in their learning journeys, the more likely they are to be engaged and motivated.

Blended learning provides a pathway for teachers looking to plan and implement learning experiences that align with the principle of providing multiple means of engagement. Teachers can use the time, space, and flexibility afforded by blended learning models to increase student engagement by teaching self-regulation skills, fostering communication and collaboration among a community of learners, and prioritizing student agency.

PROVIDE MULTIPLE MEANS OF REPRESENTATION. The second principle of UDL reminds educators to provide multiple pathways to build knowledge and comprehension in all learners. Not all learners comprehend information in the same way, have the same prior knowledge and life experiences, or have access to the same vocabulary. There must be multiple access and entry points so all students can grow as learners as they reach toward the same goal.

When presenting information, teachers often use a single representation and provide the same lesson to all students. This may be done by giving a lecture, playing a video, conducting a lab, teaching vocabulary, etc. Because there is significant variability among students, the information they need to gather before applying it in an authentic assessment will also differ. By providing multiple opportunities to learn information, we empower learners to personalize how they build knowledge and hone skills. That is easier to accomplish if the information is presented in multiple modalities that invite a degree of student agency, or choice, and if the information can be manipulated or customized by the student.

Teachers can design a choice board or use a hyperdoc to present information in multiple modalities that invite the students to engage with information in a format that appeals to or is more accessible for them. For example, teachers can provide students with the option to read a digital text, listen to a podcast or audio recording, watch a video, or analyze an infographic.

In addition to allowing students to engage with information in a variety of formats, it is helpful if students can manipulate the information they are interacting with to make it more accessible. This is easier to do when teachers make that information available digitally. For example, if teachers are using the flipped classroom model and making videos available online, students can pause, rewind, or rewatch that video explanation. They can also slow down the speed of a YouTube video or access closed captioning to improve their experience.

When information is presented in language, symbols, or visual formats, teachers should keep in mind that not all students will have the same understanding or interpretation of that information. A student's cultural background or prior knowledge may impact their level of understanding or their specific interpretation of a word, symbol, or image. The following strategies can help teachers to improve both the clarity and comprehensibility of the information presented in a class.

- Frontload, or pre-teach, vocabulary and symbols
- Help students orient their new learning in a larger context by making connections between their previous learning and the new information
- Present important information and key concepts using more than one form of media

The principle of providing multiple means of representation is easier to accomplish when teachers use blended learning models and online resources to capitalize on the affordances available in digital learning environments.

PROVIDE MULTIPLE MEANS OF ACTION AND EXPRESSION. It is not enough to comprehend information if there is no way to express it. Learners benefit from numerous methods to express their understanding as they develop into writers and speakers in developmentally appropriate ways that embrace emerging technologies.

Traditionally, students were asked to share their understanding using only one means of action, say the five-paragraph essay written in blue or black ink. Yet teachers know that not all students thrive expressing their ideas in writing. Students have different strengths and limitations, so asking them to express their ideas in a single way will not allow all students to effectively showcase what they've learned or share what they know. It is critical to think about offering students agency when it comes to expression.

Instead of requiring that all students surface their ideas or learning in the same way, teachers should consider providing various avenues from which students can choose. For example, teachers can design a project choice board or invite students to complete a project proposal describing how they would enjoy sharing their learning. This choice allows students to select a strategy for communicating their ideas that is comfortable for them. It also yields a variety of products, which will be more interesting for teachers reviewing student work.

When teachers provide multiple options, learners are able to practice executive functioning skills as they analyze the task and choose the best option to demonstrate that they met the intended outcome.

Essentially, the principles drive design by rooting the design of teaching and learning with three core questions:

- What do all learners need to know or be able to do?
- Based on variability, what barriers may prevent students from learning?
- How do I design flexible, blended pathways for all learners to learn and share what they know?

When we address these questions through design and recognize the power of student variability, flexibility, and "firm goals, flexible means," we create learning environments that value and foster expert learning.

The UDL Guidelines is a tool used in the implementation of Universal Design for Learning. The guidelines provide further considerations for each of the UDL principles and help to unpack the options to reduce or eliminate barriers to learning.[11] Although there are nine guidelines expanded within twenty-seven checkpoints, no required number of checkpoints need to be included for the instruction to be considered UDL-based.[12] It is, however, critical that educators provide options to eliminate barriers to learning.

It is important to note that "options" and "choices" are often used interchangeably, but they are not always synonymous. Too often, teachers give students options, but they do not give them choices. Students know what their options are. They know they can learn from books, videos, or teacher lectures, or by exploring resources on their own or with peers, but often they don't have a choice. Teacher lesson plans and scripted curriculum often dictate that all students read, watch a video, or attend a lecture, but students don't have choices, and therefore many of these options are not accessible or engaging.

As we have highlighted in this section, agency is a key benefit of blended learning. In order for learning to feel relevant and engaging, students must make key decisions about their learning—what they learn, how they learn, and what they want to create to demonstrate their learning. Offering meaningful choices to learners is easier to do when educators are not designing lockstep learning experiences for the entire class.

The same is true with assessments. Our students know of the countless options available, from traditional tests to essays to podcasts to community-based, project-based learning. Throughout the year, many teachers provide these options at one time or another, yet few provide students with choices while focusing on the same firm goal. Making choices is a far more rigorous cognitive task than passively accepting an option, and making choices truly captures the essence of what it means to be a learner.

Baking My Way to Expert Learning

Katie

One of my best friends, Kate, is a phenomenal baker. Every cupcake, cookie, and cake she makes is like something out of the Food Network kitchen—moist, crunchy, chewy, and just as it should be.

I, on the other hand, am no expert baker. My cookies are flat, my brownies are dry, and I only make cake from a box. I know why. It's not worth the effort for me. I rarely measure with the precision baking requires. I don't invest in high-quality ingredients. I just don't love sweets that much, and early on, I decided cooking was not what got me excited. (It may have to do with my family's lackluster reactions to the "spaghetti pie" I baked for them in seventh grade!)

If I wanted to become a baker, I could definitely move in that direction by relying on expert learning. For example, I know I am not a natural at pairing ingredients. Recipes would be my first scaffold. I don't like having gadgets in my kitchen (a real barrier to baking), but I recognize that investing in the right tools (or borrowing them from Kate) would assist me with mixing, frosting, and decorating. I would need to be more careful in my approach: don't substitute ingredients; sift my flour; level my dry measurements with a knife. I know this because I have made mistakes with baking and learned from those mistakes.

The Power of Expert Learning

Expert learning is not about being good at everything. It's about focusing on your individual needs, knowing your strengths and weaknesses, and relying on support in areas where you aren't as strong. It's about doing things the way you need to do them to reach your highest level of success. Expert learners are:

- purposeful and motivated
- resourceful and knowledgeable
- strategic and goal-directed

An expert learner may not be the best student or have the most innate talent, but that doesn't matter. An expert learner is motivated and gritty, perseveres through problems, learns from mistakes, and keeps on trying new strategies until goals are achieved. This creative problem solving is sometimes called "twenty-first-century thinking," and a student who uses it may be described as being "future-ready." We are always amused by these terms since they imply that good problem-solvers and critical thinkers didn't exist before our time. The Einsteins, Edisons, and Graham Bells of the world were always expert learners, as they were the original design thinkers and continued to tinker, take risks, and make mistakes until they reached their goal. How do we design blended learning environments so all learners have equal opportunities to explore, reflect, build, create, and learn?

What UDL Is Not

It's not enough to know what UDL is. We also want to examine what UDL isn't. UDL is not just good teaching. It is good learning. There is no variable more critical for student success than the quality of teachers. Without a doubt, the best investment a school can make is in its human resources. Just as educational philosopher and psychologist

John Dewey penned in *How We Think*, "One might as well say he has sold when no one has bought, as to say that he has taught when no one has learned."[13] Teaching is the foundation of learning, and so when we have so many students who are not successful in school, who are not independent learners, or who aren't prepared for their future, we have to reevaluate what good teaching is.

To examine how "good practice" changes, let's examine an example from the medical field. The lobotomy was introduced in 1935 by the Portuguese neurologist António Egas Moniz as a way to treat violent behavior and mental illness. Egas Moniz won the Nobel Prize in 1949 for this breakthrough. By 1984, the American Psychological Association reported that many individuals with lobotomies had been reduced to life in a nonresponsive state and required constant care. By the late 1980s, the surgery had become a mark of malpractice. How did an operation go from being worthy of the Nobel Prize to being unthinkable in less than forty years?

Teaching and learning have evolved in much the same way. As new research is published and technology evolves, we begin to see that some of our practices are signs of "malpractice." We learn more about the best way to increase student learning, and those methods change over time and are incredibly contextual. Being flexible and aligning to the core beliefs about UDL is critical to support learners.

When UDL and blended learning are successful, learners truly have ownership in their learning, as opposed to permission to make choices. One great resource to exemplify this is the UDL Progression Rubric.[14] In the excerpt shown in table 1.1, you will notice some "good teaching" strategies, where teachers offer options and choices to students, are only identified in the "emerging" UDL category.

	Emerging	Proficient	Progressing toward Expert Practice
Optimize individual choice and autonomy	Offer choices in what students learn (e.g., "choose a country to study" rather than "study France"), how students learn (e.g., use books, videos, and/or teacher instruction to build understanding), and how they express what they know (e.g., "you can create a poster or write a paragraph").	Encourage students to choose from multiple options to determine what they learn (guided by standards), how they learn, and how they express what they know. Encourage students to suggest additional options if they can still meet the standard.	Empower students to make choices or suggest alternatives for what they will learn, how they will learn, and how they will express what they know in authentic ways. Free them to self-monitor and reflect on their choices with teacher facilitation and feedback but not explicit direction.

Table 1.1: Excerpt from UDL Progression Rubric

UDL is all about learning, and UDL implementation is only approaching an expert level when *all* students, regardless of variability, are capable of setting goals and creating pathways to meet those goals. In a nutshell, while following UDL best practices is good teaching, good teaching isn't always universally designed instruction.

Myth #1: There's No Place for Direct Instruction in UDL

It is important to note that implementing UDL and blended learning does not mean that there is no direct instruction. All too often, educators think that there is no place for direct or explicit instruction in a UDL classroom. Direct instruction will always have a place in education, but the way direct instruction is delivered through UDL is quite different. To support the direct instruction, teachers provide students with choices to help support their learning and offer multiple ways to dive deeper into the information covered through direct instruction, for example by giving a student the option to read a chapter in a book, watch a video, discuss the concepts with a peer, or dive into an experiment. Whichever option the student chooses, there will be resources available to help them through struggles, such as scaffolds and exemplars. There will be frequent reminders about the goals of the lesson and classroom norms to support students with finding resources when they are challenged. So, while a lesson may incorporate mini-lessons and direct instruction, UDL encourages teachers to go beyond the "sage on the stage" role and help students take charge of their own learning.

Blended learning models also integrate direct instruction; similar to UDL, the goal is not to provide the same instruction in the same way for all students. If teachers want to provide a foundational explanation or model a strategy that all students are likely to benefit from, they can flip their instruction and record a video. The video gives students more control over the pace they move through the instruction (e.g., pausing, rewinding, rewatching). Teachers can also show students how to add closed captioning or slow down the pace of a YouTube video by adjusting the settings. The ability to manipulate visual media is likely to make this instruction more accessible for all students.

Blended learning models move away from whole-group instruction and instead prioritize small-group and personalized instruction. Teachers know that it can be challenging to hold the attention of a class full of students, let alone meet their various needs with a single explanation, mini-lesson, or lecture. As we have emphasized, learner variability is the rule, so a single explanation or model will not address the range of skills, abilities, language proficiencies, etc., in a classroom.

Blended learning provides avenues to reimagine instruction. For example, the station rotation model provides a structure for breaking the larger class into smaller groups to provide that teacher-led experience where the teacher can adjust the explanations, scaffolds and supports, and academic rigor of problems and prompts to increase the effectiveness of these direct instruction sessions. Similarly, teachers can use the playlist model or choice boards to create time in class to work with small groups of students or individual learners to provide additional support, reteaching, or guided practice. The models are designed to be flexible and create more opportunities for the teacher to connect with learners.

Myth #2: Differentiated Instruction Equates UDL

Another misconception about UDL is that it is the same thing as differentiated instruction (DI). UDL and DI are built on fundamentally different values of who is in charge of a student's learning. The primary goal of UDL is to create expert learners. UDL honors student variability and removes barriers to student learning by creating flexible pathways for students to self-differentiate their learning and to select the supports and scaffolds they believe will help them be successful.

When teachers differentiate instruction, they are responsive to individual student needs.[15] Differentiation is a teacher move, or something we do as we design instruction, to get closer to meeting the needs of individual learners or small groups of learners. For example, if you differentiate instruction, you may take one group of students aside and assign them a more challenging task, problem set, or prompt. Or you may reduce the number of tasks struggling students need to complete or vary the time they have to complete a task.

These frameworks complement each other in a multitiered system, but first, best instruction should be designed using the principles of UDL. When evidence suggests that students need additional support, intervention, or enrichment, teachers can differentiate instruction to supplement, not supplant, universally designed learning experiences.

As teachers identify the students who need *more*, they can leverage blended learning models to provide that additional support, intervention, or enrichment. Differentiation is a key benefit of blended learning. It is easier for teachers to effectively and consistently differentiate when they are not relying exclusively on a whole-group teacher-led lesson. Instead, teachers universally designing blended learning will want to build mechanisms into their lessons to collect formative assessment data. That will help them to understand where students are in terms of their understanding of key concepts and mastery of specific skills as they progress through a learning experience. That evidence or data can help teachers to identify areas of strength as well as the gaps and misconceptions that need to be addressed. Teachers can then pull students into a small group as part of a blended lesson and provide the additional instruction, reteaching, models, scaffolds, and tiered practice necessary to ensure that all students are making progress, as pictured in figure 1.6.

Universally Design Learning
- Use the principles of UDL to honor learner variability, provide firm goals with flexible means, and develop expert learners
  - Engagement
  - Representation
  - Action + Expression

Differentiate the Learning
- Provide feedback in response to formative assessment data
- Provide additional supports and scaffolds (e.g., guided note template, concept map, word bank, sentence frames, deconstructed model)
- Use flexible groupings to allow for peer support

Collect Formative Assessment Data
- Build mechanisms into the lesson to gauge understanding and progress
- Interpret the evidence or data
- Identify the gaps or areas of need

Figure 1.6: The Complementary Nature of UDL and DI

All students deserve access to rigorous, authentic, engaging learning that meets their needs. Given the incredible variability of the learners we serve, one-size-fits-all solutions will not work. Universal design provides us with a framework to approach planning with engagement and expert learning in mind. Implementing the UDL principles using blended learning models ensures that we are leveraging evidence-based instruction, innovative practices, and the promise of technology. Our educational landscape is changing. Building one skill set for face-to-face instruction and another for online learning is not necessary. Rather, we need to build a skill set that can navigate from online to offline and back again.

SUMMARIZE, REFLECT, AND DISCUSS

The goal of school is not, and has never been, to achieve high test scores and grade point averages. These are results that come when our students develop into expert, engaged learners—not the destination of education; in other words, these are signposts on the journey. We invite you on this journey to learn about the power and promise of UDL to design blended learning that meets the needs of all students in inclusive, equitable classrooms.

- The concept of "universal" is that we can design a lesson, focused on the same firm goals, with enough flexibility that it will work for all learners. In your practice, how do you currently create flexibility so all learners are challenged and supported?

- Blended learning creates flexible pathways for time and place, pace, and path. Which of these components will come most naturally to you? Which ones would be the most challenging?

- Reflecting on your own experiences is helpful in creating a strategy for moving forward. Consider challenges you may face and take notes on forthcoming chapters when you see strategies that will help you to push your practice forward.

- We've used the ski birthday party analogy to highlight the importance of "firm goals, flexible means." Think about other examples in your own life where you need to offer "flexible means" to ensure you're meeting the needs of all your family or friends. Keeping this analogy in mind may be helpful throughout your design process.

CHAPTER 2

Equity and Access

In May 2013, a video of a student, Jeff Bliss, complaining about "frickin' packets," went viral. The student was captured on video telling his teacher, "If you would just get up and teach 'em instead of handin 'em a frickin packet, yo!" Jennifer Gonzalez from *Cult of Pedagogy* beautifully reflected on why the video was so hard-hitting. She noted:

> What I have gleaned about Jeff Bliss from the internet is that at the time of the video, he was an 18-year-old sophomore. So apparently, at some point, he had not been successful in school. For some people, this takes away his credibility. For me, it makes him an even better source of information about why school isn't working for some students.
>
> Disruptive behavior aside, the content of Bliss's outburst tells me that his teacher's primary mode of instruction is through packets. This was what got me. This is what made me watch this video six, seven, eight times over. Because I just believe him.[1]

We all know that school doesn't work for all students, especially those students who have been traditionally marginalized. Our Black, brown, and Indigenous students, English language learners, students who are economically disadvantaged, LGBTQ+ students, and students with disabilities need us to abandon traditional practices to provide all students with equal opportunities to be successful. The reason our systems don't work is because there are far too many barriers in classrooms and schools that prevent students from learning.

Handing out packets is alterable—yet it is still common practice. Sites like Teachers Pay Teachers and Pinterest highlight worksheets and packets as one-size-fits-all practices that can change education. While they may make the life of teachers easier and can be incredibly fun for some learners, one-size-fits-all solutions can't change outcomes for our students because they are not designed to do that.

When we design lessons, we sometimes create structures where all learners are given "equal" methods to learn and share what they know. But not all kids are dealt the same set of cards. When we focus on equity and expert learning, we provide learners with the support they need to be successful by removing barriers. Some kids may need more support, and others may need less, to put them all on equal ground. That's okay. But it's not enough for us, who have the power and privilege to make choices for students, to make these decisions without the partnership of our learners.

Equality vs. Equity

To ensure equitable opportunities for learning, it is critical to understand the differences between equality and equity. Equality is the belief that all people have equal value as individuals and should, therefore, have equal inputs and outcomes, or one-size-fits-all experiences. In short, equality is equal distribution, where everyone gets the same thing. When focused on equality, we, as educators, have the same high expectations for all students and provide them with the same goals, materials, and assessments, as if providing students with the same high quality of education will result in equal outputs.

The problem with this is that no educator could possibly argue that what we have been doing has resulted in "common fates" for any of our students.[2]

Equity, by comparison, is focused on productivity, or ensuring that everyone has what they need to be successful. This "fair distributive principle" means that some learners will need significantly more inputs to have the same, or similar, outputs as others.[3] The conflict here is that some people perceive equity as unjust because they feel they deserve an equal share.

One saying we use in UDL is "What is necessary for some is good for all." That is not to say that all accommodations will benefit all learners, but rather, instructional scaffolds and supports, as well as options for acceleration and enrichment, should be provided as options for all. When we design through the lens of UDL, we are always looking for potential barriers that can exclude learners. Once we can identify the barriers, we need to eliminate them by providing additional, more flexible pathways, resources, and support. This is different than a teacher making decisions about which students need support and which need more challenge. As we shared previously, responding to student needs individually or with small-group instruction through differentiated instruction is critical for student learning and should supplement universally designed instruction. It cannot, however, replace it.

Transitioning to a model where students have the autonomy to make choices about their learning ensures equitable access and more equitable opportunities to learn. Some educators struggle with the concept of "what is necessary for some is good for all." Let us provide a math example to explain. Imagine a math teacher is focused on solving algebraic equations.

If a teacher were to begin with differentiated instruction, students would be placed in instructional groupings for Tier 1 instruction. Some students would receive easier problems, or remedial work, while other students are given more rigorous problems. If you're reading this scenario, you may struggle to see what is inequitable about providing learners with a curriculum that aligns with their instructional level. Clearly, additional challenge is necessary for some learners, while other learners need more support. You will not find a UDL practitioner who will argue with that. What is inequitable is that some students, in this model, are excluded from grade-level rigor and the same opportunities offered to their peers. Also problematic is that students don't have a voice, or an opportunity to determine what they need to be successful.

When using the principles of UDL, the teacher first identifies potential barriers that would prevent students from engaging with and solving algebraic equations aligned to grade-level standards. For example, some students may struggle with math facts, lack vocabulary for a meaningful explanation, or may not understand how to solve the problem while other students may not be challenged by grade-level equations. This is where "what is necessary for some is good for all" comes into play.

When universally designing a lesson, a teacher would ensure there were numerous options and choices to support learners, including access to a calculator, math reference sheets, opportunities to collaborate, a word bank, "done problems" to use as models, and opportunities to work with the teacher in small groups. Additionally, the teacher would ensure there are more challenging problems, opportunities to apply mathematics, and enrichment opportunities. All of these supports, scaffolds, and challenges would be provided as options for all learners. Think of them as a buffet of resources.

When we share this scenario with teachers, there are two pressure points that we often hear: 1) But what about the students who don't need the support? I don't want them relying on resources and taking the easy way out, and 2) There are some learners who can't do the difficult problems. I don't want to overwhelm them by providing the additional challenge.

In both of these scenarios, teachers are not confident that students can be expert learners, who can set goals, challenge themselves, and use the resources necessary to meet those goals. There is also an assumption that we know learners better than they know themselves. We don't. All learners can become expert learners if given the opportunity to choose options and reflect on those options. When we create a classroom where we can meet with individual students and small groups, in addition to providing them with universally designed blended learning options, we can help to foster expert learning by providing feedback and supporting student reflection.

In the scenarios above, there is an assumption that scaffolds, supports, and accommodations should only be available to some students when that is simply not the case. Because of variability, what students need is ever-changing and evolving. We need to give learners the opportunity every day to learn which resources are available and use the ones they need. In truth, some of these accommodations may not have been designed for learners who use them, but they benefit them all the same.

In the universally designed math lesson, students are given an exit ticket where they have to solve an algebraic equation and share their strategy for solving it via a video recording or a written explanation. Once the teacher reflects on the results of the assessments, she creates a station rotation model with flexible groups based on the data from the formative assessment. The teacher will work with each group to target intervention, feedback, and enrichment. While the teacher is working with each group, other students are working through stations that combine on-demand video instruction and models, review and practice, and online discussions.

One analogy to explain the concept of "what is necessary for some is good for all" is the delivery option at local stores and restaurants.

Let's take your local pizza shop. It may offer delivery. Why? Because the owner wants to make sure that no one is excluded from buying food. The owner can predict that some people lack transportation and they need the delivery option. Here's the thing—the delivery isn't only offered to people who don't have transportation. Can you imagine the absurdity of a place saying, "Oh, you have a car? Sorry, we don't offer delivery. Take the hard road, get in your car, and march yourself into the shop to get your eggplant parmesan." That would be quite the way to lose business!

Instead, we all have the option to choose delivery, just as we all have the option to pay with cash or credit card, choose our pizza toppings, and choose carryout or eat-in. When we recognize and embrace variability, we create options, and then we allow learners (and diners!) to think about their current circumstances and choose what they need. That is equity.

In 1997, the New Teacher Project (TNTP) was founded by teachers who believed all students were capable of learning at high levels and deserved great teaching. TNTP recently published the findings of a multiyear study that followed four thousand students in five diverse school systems to learn more about their experiences. What they found was sobering. The report, dubbed "The Opportunity Myth," shared:

> Most students—and especially students of color, those from low-income families, those with mild to moderate disabilities, and English language learners—spent the vast majority of their school days missing out on four crucial resources: grade-appropriate assignments, strong instruction, deep engagement, and teachers with high expectations. Students spent more than 500 hours per school year on assignments that weren't appropriate for their grade and with instruction that didn't ask enough of them—the

equivalent of six months of wasted class time in each core subject.[4]

Educators around the globe have the amazing privilege and challenge to create schools that work for all students. Although we have made great strides in the past few decades with increasing inclusion rates, implementing Universal Design for Learning and blended learning in pockets, and adopting whole-school initiatives like restorative justice, the reality is we are *still* not meeting the needs of many of our students, and our teaching styles, curriculum, classrooms, schools, and districts need to change.

The goal of a universally designed system is to create a Tier 1 environment that is the least restrictive and most culturally responsive and trauma-informed environment for all students. Too often, Tier 1 general education classrooms are perceived to be "restrictive" because of outdated, one-size-fits-all pedagogy that was designed for the mythical average learner. If a school or district is looking to create a system where high-quality tiered support is offered in addition to, and not instead of, Tier 1 support, they must provide equitable access to all students through Universal Design for Learning and blended learning.

Providing access to learning is the lowest bar. Every child deserves a "seat" in the classroom with their peers and a high-quality teacher who teaches grade-level standards. Equitable access means every student gets that seat in the classroom with their peers, regardless of variability, disabilities, barriers, or the learning landscape. In schools, we are always trying to address barriers that students face academically, behaviorally, socially, and emotionally. Although these barriers may be very different, we need to address them in the same way—by providing learners with flexible options and choices they need to be engaged, supported, and motivated to learn.

Empathy Exercises

At TEDxTeachersCollege, Dr. Christopher Emdin, a professor and equity expert, defined equity as "hearing somebody's voice about what they need and providing them with that."[5] So how do we do that?

One effective practice to build more equitable classrooms is to carve out time for empathy exercises. As one participant in a large-scale study noted, "Empathy is the first step to getting toward equity . . . It's impossible to meet the needs of a person without understanding them."[6] To design learning that authentically meets the needs of our learners, we have to understand and listen *before* we design.

Empathy exercises are drawn from the field of design thinking. Stanford University has a world-renowned school of design, dubbed the d.school. The d.school's *Design Thinking Bootleg*, a manual that outlines the design process, identifies empathy as the first step of design. *The Design Thinking Bootleg* reminds us that to empathize with our "users," or, in our case, learners, we have to "interact with and interview them. Engaging users reveals deeper insights into their beliefs and values."[7]

In *The Innovator's Mindset*, our friend George Couros identified eight characteristics of an innovative mindset. The first is empathy. Couros writes, "Empathetic teachers think about the classroom environment and learning opportunities from the point of view of the student, not the teacher."[8] In order to create equitable opportunities to learn, and to be more innovative, we have to build empathy and learn from our students. The d.school has some sage advice about these empathy exercises: "Listen. Really. Ditch any agendas and let the scene soak into your psyche. Absorb what users say to you, and how they say it, without thinking about how you're going to respond."[9]

When students are struggling, we have an incredible opportunity to interview them and learn more about their lives, their experiences, their perspectives, and what they need from schools. When scheduling empathy exercises, it's important to remember the principles of UDL and how flexibility is key. Provide printed copies of the questions ahead of time so students have time to reflect, and provide an opportunity for students to write answers, record videos, or meet in person or virtually. The firm goal is elevating and celebrating the voices of learners. The means, of course, are flexible.

A book Katie coauthored, *Equity by Design: Delivering on the Promise of UDL*, discusses the importance of these student conversations, or empathy interviews, as a strategy to build more equitable and accessible learning environments.[10] We have a responsibility to share the goals of our classroom and then meet with students individually and in small groups to help us design learning with pathways that are "necessary for some and good for all." The following questions are starting points for conversations about teaching and learning:

- What do you think you need to know or do to be able to meet this goal?
- How would you best like to learn it?
- What materials can I provide you that will help you to meet this goal?
- How will you share that you met it?

Empathy interviews are not only important in learning design, but throughout the year as we commit to continuous improvement. To do this, we can implement what Dr. Christopher Emdin refers to as cogenerative dialogues, or "cogens." Emdin shares, "Cogens are simple conversations between the teacher and their students with a goal of co-creating/generating plans of action for improving the classroom."[11] Cogens welcome student self-expression and value the voices of students as well as critiques of the classroom with the aim of creating more meaningful and equitable learning for all students.

If we want to create equal opportunities for all learners to succeed, we have to ditch our one-size-fits-all practices and provide flexible pathways for students to learn. Blended learning provides teachers with various models they can leverage to design learning experiences that meet individual and small groups of learners where they are in the learning process. As designers, we have a responsibility to our learners to learn about their strengths, their values, and what they need to be successful in our schools. When we create opportunities to listen to learners and collaborate with them, we can design more equitable learning.

However, to design equitable learning experiences using blended learning demands that all students are connected and have reliable access to a device and internet connection. Otherwise, technology-enhanced instructional models will only serve to further disenfranchise students who are economically disadvantaged. We would be remiss to not address the importance of digital technology in meeting the needs of all learners, and the importance of digital equity.

Digital Access and Equity in Online Learning

When the pandemic forced schools to close their doors in the spring of 2020 and transition to online learning, we watched public schools all over the United States freeze in a state of paralysis. Many school districts did not have current data to identify which students had reliable access to the internet or the hardware necessary to access learning online. Not only was student access a concern, many teachers did not have any training or experience teaching online. The focus in those early months was survival. The learning landscape had shifted dramatically in a matter of days and weeks. For schools that had not invested heavily in technology or professional learning focused on blended and online learning, this state of paralysis extended into summer. The final months of the 2019–2020 school year were lost in the general chaos created by the pandemic and concerns about access and equity.

Digital Access and Privilege

Catlin

As a parent of two children enrolled in our local public school system, I had a front-row seat to the challenges facing our educational institutions. Despite living in one of the wealthiest states in America, I watched as California's public school system grappled with this shift online. Issues of equity and access dominated conversations. There was a fear that requiring students to join synchronous classes via videoconference was going to exacerbate the deep divides that already existed in our school system. In a policy and practice brief published by the California Collaborative on District Reform, the authors acknowledged the state's limited experience with distance learning and lack of both human capacity and a coherent online instructional program.[12]

Even though the shift online was rocky, my children have adapted and are doing well because of their privilege. They each have a Chromebook for their exclusive use at home. They have a reliable internet connection. They have two parents willing and able to support them in navigating assignments. Unfortunately, that is not the case for every child. The pandemic shone a spotlight on the myriad inequities that exist for so many learners. First and foremost was the issue of digital access, which is defined as "an individual's ability to obtain tools such as computers and smartphones, as well as consistent connection to the internet."[13] Without access to a computer and the internet, how were students going to learn from home?

I received a digital survey about our digital access from my kids' school two weeks into the shelter-in-place order that closed schools in March. I remember thinking, *Why wasn't this data collected at the start of every school year?* Our school district quickly realized that a significant number of students and families would not be able to access learning online. I watched as our school district, along with many others, scrambled to get families packets of handouts and offline work, deliver mobile hotspots, and distribute devices that had previously lived in Chromebook carts in classrooms on campus. As I watched this mobilization of resources, I could not help but think that at the very least one silver lining of the pandemic was that more (though not all) students and families would have digital access.

Beyond Digital Access

Equity issues extend far beyond digital access. Socioeconomic and familial inequities also became more apparent as students learned remotely from home. Not all home environments are conducive to learning. The debate that raged about whether or not students should have cameras turned on during videoconferencing sessions and the expectation that they be seated at a desk in a quiet space in their homes unearthed some of the deep disparities in our students' home lives. The cameras on our students' devices provide a window into their lives, their homes, and their family dynamics that they may not want to share. Yes, seeing our students' faces makes our jobs easier, but it is a vulnerable position for many students. Many students are sharing space with family members or juggling the demands of caring for younger siblings. That doesn't even account for the students who may be experiencing home insecurity and lack a stable home environment from which to log in to their classes. All of these factors create barriers to learning online for many students.

Los Angeles Unified School District (LAUSD) released data about student engagement online, which showed that 6–10 percent of students who are English learners, students with disabilities, students experiencing homelessness, and students in foster care never logged onto the LAUSD online learning platform from March to May of 2020.[14] According to Bellwether Education Partners, a national nonprofit, approximately three million students in the United States have dropped out of school since March 2020. The most disturbing part of this data is that this number is just an estimate based on the scant data available. The actual number of students no longer engaged in learning could be much higher. The long-term impacts of a disruption in a child's education are vast, impacting their "knowledge and skills, achievement, path to college and career, and lifetime wages."[15] Research suggests that once a student drops out of school they are unlikely to reenroll, or if they do, they are unlikely to stay enrolled and graduate.[16]

Issues of equity and access are complex and multifaceted, but they demand our attention if we expect students to navigate flexible learning landscapes. If students are going to learn both in class and online, leaders must continue the important work of closing the digital divide and get every student digital access. Currently, 3.6 million households in the United States do not have a computer (e.g., laptop, desktop, or tablet), which means that 7.3 million students are attempting to meet the demands of online learning with a small smartphone screen that has limited capability, or they are without a device entirely.[17] Access to hardware can be addressed by allocating funds to purchasing hardware for students who do not have a device at home. Many school districts have focused on device deployment to ensure all students have a computer they can use for online learning.

Access to high-speed internet is a harder issue for school districts to tackle and requires more state and federal funding to address. A national analysis found that "34 percent of American Indian/Alaska Native families and about 31 percent each of Black and Latino families lack access to high-speed home internet compared to only 21 percent of White families."[18] It's clear from the data that the lack of access to home internet is disproportionately impacting communities of color, making it more challenging for students in those communities to be successful.

As daunting as issues of equity and access are, educational institutions must be prepared to tackle them head-on. We cannot afford to lose students from educational institutions because they cannot get connected or do not have access to a device that allows them to successfully navigate online learning. In addition, students need access to academically rigorous, mentally stimulating, and differentiated learning opportunities provided by trained teachers who know how to leverage the benefits of both online and offline learning to provide students with a high-quality educational experience regardless of the learning landscape. Universal Design for Learning combined with blended learning offers educators and educational institutions a path forward.

Blended Learning Grounded in Equity

As we have shared throughout this text, we need to move away from providing all students with the same experiences, and instead, we need to find ways to partner with students and families, understand their individual needs, and remove the barriers facing each child. In an interview published by Edutopia, Dr. Pedro Noguera, an expert in educational equity, encourages society more generally and educators specifically to "see" the inequities that exist and stop ignoring them. He believes that acknowledging inequity is the first step in reimagining and reorganizing education to transition from "talking at kids" to more interactive and applied learning. He makes the powerful point that "you don't have to change the kids or their culture" to change outcomes; instead we have to change the conditions in schools.[19]

The iNACOL Blended Learning Teacher Competency Framework is grounded in three essential beliefs about learning. First, blended learning teachers must have a strong commitment to high expectations and be committed to achieving equitable outcomes for *all* students. Second, blended learning teachers must have a desire to move toward a competency-based approach to learning that recognizes that students learn at different paces and assessment should be used strategically. Third, blended learning teachers must value all students, "including those with different skills, exceptionalities, and needs."[20]

A blended learning teacher understands that the input each student needs to achieve equitable outcomes will be different. This demands that teachers know their students and work alongside them to provide the support necessary to achieve equitable outcomes. It isn't about teaching to that mythical average student, or lowering expectations for particular groups of learners. Blended learning acknowledges and celebrates variability and strives to provide personalized learning experiences that give each student exactly what they need to thrive academically.

Embracing Student Funds of Knowledge

If we want to reimagine education and create more equitable opportunities for all students to learn, we need to embrace a competency-based, personalized approach. Universally designed blended learning provides a path for educators and educational institutions to shift control over the time, place, pace, and path of learning to students and to help them to develop the skills necessary to thrive in any learning landscape. To do this well, we have to get to know our students, their identities, their strengths, and their limitations and recognize the importance of designing flexible options with them in mind. When we do this, it reflects a belief that all learners have value.

The strength of an equitable learning community lies in its diversity. The funds of knowledge, life experience, cultural backgrounds, family structures, religious beliefs, skills and abilities, and linguistic diversity in a learning community add depth and richness. The funds of knowledge framework has been used to research the "competence and knowledge embedded in the life experiences of under-represented students and their families."[21] Funds of knowledge are the "historically accumulated and culturally developed bodies of knowledge and skills essential for household or individual functioning and well-being."[22] Our students come from unique home environments and enter school with knowledge and skills that have been honed in those environments and influenced by their culture, family connections, social networks, and socioeconomic status. Students may have many informal teachers in their home environments who have helped them to develop cognitive and cultural resources and skills. Teachers must find ways to tap into these funds of knowledge and capitalize on them in the classroom to design culturally relevant learning experiences. This is easier to do when teachers create opportunities for students to share what they know or can do and when they invite families into the learning experience (e.g., by making home visits, hosting classroom events, and inviting parents to join the class to share their expertise on a topic). The more we value and celebrate the diversity in our classes, the more evident it is that we must move away from the classic one-size-fits-all approach to designing and facilitating learning.

SUMMARIZE, REFLECT, AND DISCUSS

All students deserve equitable access to teaching and learning that holds them to high expectations and meets their needs academically, behaviorally, socially, emotionally, linguistically, and culturally. Given the evolving learning landscapes, and the power and promise of digital tools and technology, ensuring that all students and families have digital access and high-quality devices is a moral imperative. Schools and districts must create strategic plans that ensure equal access to learning. But access alone is not equity.

In addition to access to high-quality learning, practitioners have to think differently about design. Designing one-size-fits-all experiences excludes many of the learners we serve. A universally designed approach to blended learning that seeks to shift control over the learning experience from the teacher to the students will also help learners to cultivate skills, like self-regulation, self-direction, communication, collaboration, critical thinking, and creative problem-solving. These skills will serve students well regardless of their paths beyond school.

- "The Opportunity Myth" shares that many students lack access to four key drivers for success: grade-appropriate assignments, strong instruction, deep engagement, and teachers with high expectations. How do UDL and blended learning ensure that all learners have access to these critical drivers?

- This chapter discusses the difference between equality and equity. In your own words, describe the difference between the two concepts. Next, identify practices in your learning environment that are focused on equality, and others that align more closely to equity.

- The digital divide creates barriers for many learners in flexible learning landscapes. How has your school or district worked to eliminate the digital divide? Are there any additional steps you could advocate for?

CHAPTER 3

Design:
Kicking One-Size-Fits-All to the Curb

Want to Borrow My Heels?

Katie

I love high heels, especially in bright, bold colors. My favorite heels are a pair of candy-apple red stilettos. Apparently, I have Louis XIV to thank for making heels fashionable, especially red ones. As rumor has it, Louis wore red heels like a badge of honor, and no one but him was allowed to wear them in court.[1] Clearly, he wasn't a big fan of inclusive practices.

Whenever a new pair is shipped to my house, I gingerly take the shoes out of the box, put them on my feet like a scene out of Cinderella, and mutter, "Hellllooooo, ladies" to the chagrin of my children. I love how heels make my legs feel strong and announce my presence with my signature clickety-clack. It's true—in any school or office where I have worked, people hear me coming before they can see me.

As it turns out, heels have quite a history. As early as the tenth century, long before the days of Louis XIV, soldiers wore heels on horseback so their feet would fit better in the stirrups. Still today, many cowboys wear heels. Stilettos, kitten heels, platforms, cowboy boots, and heeled shoes for all genders provide a myriad of options and choices.

Now, imagine that I owned the only shoe store in town, and I only sold candy-apple red heels, à la King Louis (in size 9.5, of course). How would you feel about that? Don't worry if they aren't your size. I can cut out the toe or stuff some tissues in there. Can't walk with heels? I'll teach you, and if I have to, I can rip the heels off. Don't like them? That's just too bad.

Education is a little like my shoe store. As teachers and administrators, we have teaching techniques that work for us. We have to remember, however, that they don't always work for our learners, even when we make accommodations and modifications. Here's the thing: I can't make you walk in my shoes. But I can design options and choices so everyone can get where they need to go, because let's face it: some people would drive themselves crazy with the clickety-clack. To do this, we have to become design thinkers.

Becoming Design Thinkers

IBM, a leader in Enterprise Design Thinking, shares three principles for design thinking:

- a focus on user outcomes
- diverse empowered teams
- restless reinvention[2]

USER OUTCOMES. Both of us love a nice pair of red high heels, but if we are designing footwear for you, it needs to be about what *you* need, not what *we* prefer. And yet, although it would be so much easier to share what works for us in UDL, it's critical that we embrace the variability of our learners, encourage their feedback, and, most importantly, build empathy about their experience—a critical aspect of design.

As you consider what your students need from a learning experience and where they are headed in terms of learning outcomes, you must also consider the path students will take to get there from where they are. Blended learning identifies "path" as one of the elements that students should have some control over. Since not all students start in the same place or are headed to the same location or outcome, their path must be appropriate for them.

To be fair, it's daunting from a teacher's perspective to think about how to understand where each student is starting from, identify outcomes that are appropriate for them, and help them to customize their path to ensure they are able to reach specific individual outcomes. The good news is that blended learning models offer multiple pathways to help students get to desired user outcomes. The models themselves create clear structures that educators can lean on to make flexible pathways more manageable and sustainable. Learner variability is a strength in the classroom, and we must design learning experiences that capitalize on that strength.

DIVERSE EMPOWERED TEAMS. The curriculum design process should not be done in isolation. As educators, we are called to identify barriers to learning and eliminate those barriers through design. Oftentimes, the barriers are too complex and multifaceted to be meaningfully solved alone. If we are going to provide options and choices for learners that are relevant, authentic, meaningful, linguistically appropriate, culturally sustaining, and trauma-informed, we must collaborate with our teams and our students.

In Chapter 8, we focus on the value of participating in a community of practice (CoP) to continue learning with and from other educators as we refine our practice and grow in this work. CoPs offer a collaborative approach to professional learning, community building, and addressing problems of practice and design. When small groups of educators meet regularly to reflect on instructional planning and practice, share expertise and insights from their teaching experiences, and engage in collective problem-solving, expert learning is maximized.

Similarly, when we dedicate time to conferencing with our students, we can co-create pathways that are authentically relevant. We make space for them to tell us what they need, or which shoe is going to work best for them.

Designing dynamic learning experiences is a team sport. We benefit from working with colleagues who can inspire, challenge, and support us. We must also view students as our teammates and partners if we are going to design experiences that are interesting, relevant, and engaging to them.

RESTLESS REINVENTION. The focus on restless reinvention is the essence of expert learning in UDL. We cannot teach lessons as we have in the past, and we can never settle for following a boxed curriculum as it is designed. Asking all learners to learn in the same way, at the same pace, is like us expecting everyone who reads this book to wear the same pair of shoes. It simply doesn't work. But just because one lesson is universally designed doesn't mean that we can sit back and polish our heels.

Restless reinvention and a commitment to continued learning and experimentation are not only necessary to continually improve our practice and better meet the needs of diverse populations of students, but critical to teaching in a digital world. Technology and digital media literacy are not just helpful in life beyond K-12 educational institutions, they are essential. Technology is rapidly evolving and changing the way people communicate, collaborate, create, and share. That requires that we continually reflect on and reevaluate why we are doing what we are doing, how we are doing it, and what we are hoping to achieve. As the world beyond our classroom walls continues to change and evolve, those shifts need to be mirrored in our design if we want learning to be interesting, engaging, and relevant.

When we are committed to restless reinvention, we are committed to co-designing learning experiences with our learners through a cycle of planning, inquiry, and reflection. The UDL design cycle (figure 3.1) identifies stages of design thinking that educators use to create authentic opportunities for all students to learn in flexible learning landscapes.

UDL Design Cycle

Regardless of the learning landscape you're designing for, the planning process typically entails common elements that correspond to these four components:

- identifying lesson goals and objectives that align to standards (goals)
- developing instructional strategies and blended learning models (methods)
- choosing resources, technology tools, and materials (materials)
- assessing student progress and outcomes (assessment)[3]

Reflecting on these components and how you can design blended learning in flexible learning landscapes is critical for design. Figure 3.1 illustrates the cycle of instruction, denoting how standards can guide the development of goals, which in turn guide the development of assessments, methods, and materials.

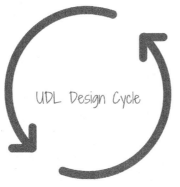

Pre-work: Identify the target
academic standard and spend time
unwrapping and understanding it

Step 6: Reflect on what worked
and what can be changed to
reduce barriers and increase
access; revise as needed

Step 1: Develop clear goal
statements in relation to the skills
and concepts in the target academic
standard

UDL Design Cycle

Step 5: Teach the standards-
based lesson(s) designed with
UDL considerations

Step 2: Develop assessments in
relation to the goals; use the UDL
guidelines to develop varied formative
and summative assessments

Step 3 + 4: Develop flexible methods
and materials. Use the UDL guidelines
to include supports and scaffolds

Figure 3.1: UDL Design Cycle

GOALS. Oftentimes, teachers create goals that include embedded methods. The UDL lesson design process begins by focusing on learner outcomes and unwrapping academic standards. Ask yourself, "What is it that all learners need to know or be able to do?" This distinction is the difference between content (to know) and methods or skills (to do). When learning content, students can be very creative about how they express their knowledge. On the other hand, if an outcome states how students will demonstrate their knowledge, it is necessary to provide support and scaffolds for students who may struggle with achieving the standard independently.

METHODS. There are multiple ways that students can learn content, build background information, and explore the knowledge and skills under study. UDL and blended learning offer students a choice of which methods they will use to learn. Provide options for the approaches, procedures, or routines that students can choose to accelerate or enhance learning. As an example, instead of lecturing to all students and then requiring the whole class to watch a video, tell them, "After a mini-lesson, you will choose to participate in small-group instruction, watch a video via Google Classroom, read a chapter in the course text, or listen to an audio version of the text." Know there is always more than one way for students to learn.

MATERIALS. Materials are usually seen as the media used to present learning content and what the learner uses to demonstrate knowledge, but oftentimes, the same materials are provided to all students. Consider setting up a menu of resources for students to choose from. Offer graphic organizers, math reference sheets, exemplars, etc. Don't require all students to use the same materials to learn and express what they know. Because of variability, they will not all need the same support, and they should be empowered to know themselves as learners and choose what they need.

ASSESSMENTS. Assessments are expressions of student learning. Assessments gather information about a learner's performance. Oftentimes, we think of these as "tests," but it can be any expression of knowledge, as illustrated in figure 3.2, that allows the educator to determine that the students can meet the goal. When designing assessments, it's critical to consider exactly what students need to know and do and then strip away any specific methods that have been tied to the goal. Essentially, when reviewing your standards, ask yourself, "How will students provide evidence that they met the goal? Can they have choices?"

The UDL flowchart[4] helps educators think about potential barriers in lesson design that prevent students from learning. Consider the components of lesson design and how each component lends itself to student self-differentiation using the principles of Universal Design for Learning and how it can be applied in a blended learning model.

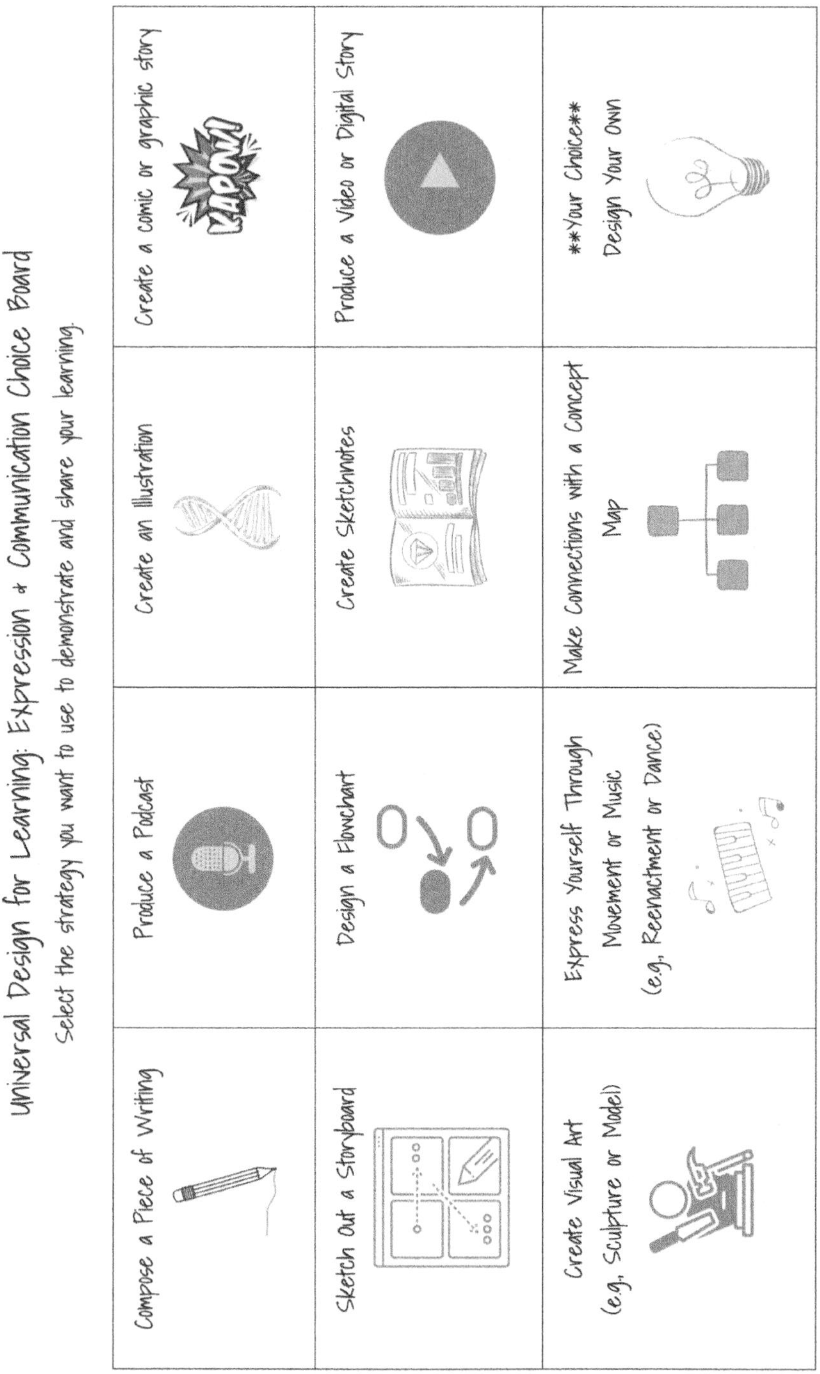

Universal Design for Learning: Expression & Communication Choice Board

Select the strategy you want to use to demonstrate and share your learning.

Compose a Piece of Writing	Produce a Podcast	Create an Illustration	Create a comic or graphic story
Sketch Out a Storyboard	Design a Flowchart	Create Sketchnotes	Produce a Video or Digital Story
Create Visual Art (e.g., Sculpture or Model)	Express Yourself Through Movement or Music (e.g., Reenactment or Dance)	Make Connections with a Concept Map	**Your Choice** Design Your Own

Figure 3.2: UDL Expression and Communication Choice Board

Architects of Learning Experiences

Catlin

After my family lost our home in the 2017 Tubbs Fire that devastated Santa Rosa, California, I had my first experience with an architect. I remember my husband and I having heated debates about whether to save money and time by rebuilding the house exactly as it was before the fire or to hire an architect to design a completely new home. The cost of working with an architect was significant, and starting from square one, in terms of design, was going to take more time.

As we thought about the house we had lost, my husband and I agreed that there was a lot about it that we would love to change. The A-line roof created slanted, low ceilings in our bedroom, there was limited closet space (and, like Katie, I loved my collection of heels), and the only showers were located upstairs, which was not ideal when our aging parents came for a visit. After some reflection, we decided the cost and time associated with designing a new home was worth it. After losing everything in the fire, we wanted to build our dream home.

I remember my first meeting with the architect. I wasn't sure what to expect when I entered his office. I figured he might show me images of different homes and ask me to identify features or characteristics I liked about each. We did not look at photographs of homes; instead, we sat in his cozy office and we talked for an hour. He wanted to understand me and my family. He probed gently with his questions to understand what we valued and how we used the space in our home. Did I cook regularly? Did we eat dinner together as a family? Did I like to sit outside? Where did we hang out in the evenings? He asked questions about the home we had lost and what I liked about it. He asked me what I wished for in a new home. He was slowly constructing a picture of our ideal home based on my answers to these questions. Although he had a legal pad and a pen, he made only a few notes. Mostly, he listened.

When we left, I wondered how the architect would take our conversation and turn those details into a home. Yet that is exactly what he did. Over the course of three meetings, he took what he learned about me and my family and designed our dream home. I learned a great deal about what it means to be an effective designer of learning experiences from the process of designing and rebuilding my home.

LISTEN TO YOUR STUDENTS AND LEARN FROM THEM. Just as the architect took time to understand me—my values, my preferences, my likes and dislikes—educators who want to design learning experiences that honor learner variability must invest time and energy into getting to know their students. Design work begins with building relationships and understanding the people we are designing for. We must strive to construct a learner profile that captures each student's "individual skills, gaps, strengths, weaknesses, interests" as well as their hopes, fears, and goals.[5] The more accurate the profile, the more effective the design will be. Personalization demands that we ask questions: "What do you need?" "What will work best for you?"

LET STUDENTS DO THE WORK. After our plans had been approved by the city, the hard work of building our home began. Although the architect created the blueprint, it was our general contractor and a variety of subcontractors who brought our home to life. Just like the architect, teachers sketch out a plan, or blueprint, for the learning experience, but it is the students, like the contractors, who must do the hard work of constructing knowledge and making meaning. This requires that students have a degree of control over time, place, and pace. Some students will work more quickly than others, accomplishing tasks in a fraction of the time it takes their peers. Some students thrive in the quiet space of a bedroom, while others prefer the buzz of background noise in a classroom, working alongside their peers. Asking all students to make meaning on the same timeline, in the same environment, and at the same pace doesn't make sense, yet that is how many classrooms operate. The disillusionment, frustration, and boredom produced by this approach creates a host of other issues and behaviors that distract from learning and make our jobs exponentially more challenging.

MAKE PEACE WITH THE MESS. Learning, like building a home, isn't a tidy affair. I remember walking through our home at various stages of the building process. The floor was littered with pieces of wood, nails, rolls of tape, tools, discarded fast-food wrappers, and empty water bottles. It was a disaster! Yet, the mess was part of the process.

Similar to builders, students need the time and space to make a mess. They need to get comfortable with experimentation, failure, iteration, and revision. To be actively engaged in the process of making meaning, students must get comfortable asking questions, exploring ideas, engaging in conversation, trying different approaches or strategies, collaborating with their peers, and creating artifacts that demonstrate what they are learning. Living through a rebuild was exhausting both mentally and emotionally, but at the end of the long, hard road was a beautiful home. I remember walking through our home and experiencing a jolt of pride that we had pulled it off.

We must remind our students that learning is hard work, but the reward of understanding complex concepts and mastering specific skills is made sweeter when we've had to struggle. We must normalize this struggle as part of the process of constructing knowledge and honing skills.

DEMONSTRATE YOUR COMMITMENT TO LEARNING WITH YOUR DESIGN. Like my decision whether to rebuild our original house or design a new home to meet my family's specific needs, teachers must decide if they are going to reuse lessons each year or design learning experiences for specific groups of students. The truth is that designing differentiated and personalized learning experiences, just like my decision to redesign my home, takes time and a higher level of intentionality. Designing learning experiences is both cognitively challenging *and* cognitively engaging. Our design work demands that we think critically and creatively about how to effectively weave together online and offline learning, prioritize student agency, and provide the necessary scaffolds to ensure all students can make progress toward learning goals. This requires a commitment to relentless reinvention.

RECOUP TIME SPENT ON DESIGN DURING THE LESSON. The time teachers invest in their design work at the front end of a learning experience should result in *more* time gained during the lesson. If we design learning experiences that place students at the center of the learning, we no longer need to feel trapped at the front of the room orchestrating the lesson. We can use this freedom to prioritize aspects of our work that are often neglected due to a lack of time.

Reteaching concepts, providing feedback, and assessing student work are critical to student success. Unfortunately, a whole-group, teacher-led design does not provide us time or space to do these things during a lesson. Instead, we may ask a student to come into class during lunch or sign up for a virtual office hour to access the additional support and reteaching they need. Similarly, feedback and assessment are aspects of our job that most teachers take home to do in their evenings or on weekends. Universally designed blended learning can provide an avenue to pull reteaching, feedback, and assessment into the classroom.

Teachers can dedicate their teacher-led station to reteaching and providing additional scaffolds or providing focused, actionable feedback as students work. They can flip their instruction or use the playlist model to create the time and space to meet with individual students to conduct side-by-side assessments so students understand what they are doing well and where they need to invest more time and energy developing. Instead of happening in isolation, giving feedback and assessing student work become opportunities for a conversation about student progress. And this is time very well spent.

Building Relationships with Learners through Conferencing

UDL is focused on ensuring that students have both choice and voice. Building relationships with learners and providing them with opportunities to share their learning experiences is critical in optimizing student voice. Additionally, spending individual time with learners allows us to connect and build meaningful relationships. Studies have shown that positive teacher-student relationships lead to a learning environment that increases student achievement and motivation to learn. In contrast, conflictual teacher-student relationships are associated with lower achievement and self-esteem.[6]

A book Catlin wrote, *Balance with Blended Learning*, encourages teachers to form a partnership with students. This teacher-learner partnership is grounded in the following principles:

- mutual respect and trust
- shared purpose and goal setting
- open and honest communication
- regular, timely feedback
- balance of power
- a commitment to learning together[7]

If teachers view their students as true partners in the learning process, they are less likely to do the lion's share of the work in classrooms. They are *more* likely to approach this work with the goal of sharing the responsibility for learning with the students. Not only does this partnership help shift control from teacher to learner, which is the goal of blended learning, but it also demands that the teacher invest time and energy into their relationships with students.

Unfortunately, the traditional, teacher-led, whole-group approach to instruction that has characterized learning for the last two hundred years does not afford teachers the time to connect with individual learners. In contrast, blended learning models by their very nature allow for more individual or small group interactions, which foster more opportunities for student voice and choice.

Conferencing with students is one of the most powerful ways to nurture this teacher-learner partnership and build an engaging learning environment. Conferencing sessions help teachers to develop trust, engage in goal setting, open the lines of communication, provide timely feedback, prioritize student agency, and demonstrate a commitment to learning, which helps to build empathy.

Conferencing can be used for a variety of purposes, which include:

- discussing student goals and progress toward learning objectives
- providing personalized instruction, support, or reteaching
- offering a 1:1 coaching session
- hosting a real-time feedback session to provide focused, actionable feedback on work in progress
- conducting a side-by-side assessment
- troubleshooting an issue or problem the student is having

Catlin has developed a four *P*s framework to guide teacher-learner conferences. The four *P*s stand for purpose, preparation, post-conference plan, and parent communication.

PURPOSE. How do students want to use this time? What would feel valuable and relevant to them? What would help them to make meaningful progress at this moment? Instead of the teacher dictating the purpose of a conferencing session, the student enjoys some choice and voice in articulating the purpose of this time together.

PREPARATION. Once the student has articulated the purpose of the conference, they must prepare. What do students need to do in advance of this conversation to prepare for the conference? Should they bring specific pieces of work or come with questions? Preparation is key to ensuring that this time is productive.

POST-CONFERENCE PLAN. What are the next steps for the student and the teacher following the conference? What will students need to do to "act" on what they learned during the conference? What additional support might the teacher need to provide? During the conference itself, it is important that the teacher and learner capture a list of "next steps," or action items.

PARENT COMMUNICATION. The final *P* in the four *P*s conference framework is looping parents or family members into the conversation about student progress. How can students communicate with their parents or guardians about the purpose of the conference and their next steps? What platform would allow them to send this update about their progress to their families (e.g., email, SMS message, voice memo)?

Think about how you can put students in charge of this communication home. Asking students to communicate regularly with families alleviates the pressure that most educators feel to keep parents and guardians abreast of how individual students are doing at all times. It also requires that students take more responsibility for their learning and progress.

The four *P*s conferencing framework provides a clear path for educators to facilitate meaningful interactions with students. The planning document, pictured in figure 3.4, provides a guide to helping students think about the purpose of this time, prepare accordingly, and capture their next steps.

STUDENT CONFERENCE				
	Pre-Conference		During the Conference	Post-Conference
	Purpose	Preparation	Post-Conference Plan	Parent Communication
What do you want to do with this time? Start by selecting the purpose of your conference. →	A) Revisit and revise goals		Student action Items: •	
	B) Focused feedback			
	C) 1:1 coaching		Teacher action items: •	
	D) Troubleshoot a problem or issue			

Figure 3.4: Four *P*s Conference Planning Document

To create time in class for conferencing sessions, teachers must design lessons that weave together online and offline learning to free them to engage in these conversations with students. They may design a station rotation lesson that does not include a teacher-led station, they can use the online time during a whole-group rotation, or they may build conferencing sessions into a playlist. The key is to value this time as critical to developing and maintaining our relationships with students. Conferencing shifts the focus of our work to supporting individual learners and personalizing their learning journeys. It emphasizes the value of human relationships and connections in the learning process.

Exemplar Lesson

Note how the lesson below, focused on narrative writing, uses the principles and components of UDL and blended learning to ensure that all students have flexible pathways to learn and share what they know. The lesson also provides teachers time to connect and conference with students, providing differentiated instruction and individual feedback. Students begin by closely reading or listening to a food memoir so they can create their own food memoir that reflects their identity and culture.

First, note how the goals, methods, materials, and assessments provide flexibility. Next, note how the UDL lesson can be used in a blended learning model.

NARRATIVE WRITING

GOAL
- Write a narrative to develop real or imagined experiences or events using effective technique, relevant descriptive details, and well-structured event sequences.

METHODS
- **Must do:** Teacher provides explicit instruction on imagery and relevant description details (10 minutes).

- **Options**—Students can choose to:
  - Watch a video on imagery
  - Review the textbook section on imagery
  - Complete a scavenger hunt to find their own examples of imagery to continue to build background knowledge

- **Must do:** Read/listen to the essay "No Woman, No Cry," (first two paragraphs), highlighting or annotating the imagery and descriptive detail.
- **Options**—You can choose to:
  - Work alone or with a partner
  - Access a hard copy of the text, listen to it, or access it digitally

MATERIALS
- Graphic organizer to support annotation
- What about this writing is particularly powerful?
- Which images (sensory details) pop out at you? What can you see, hear, smell, taste, or feel?
- What are the main events that take place in the story?

ASSESSMENTS
- Using "No Woman, No Cry" as an example of effective description, choose a food that brings back a vivid memory for you and describe it in detail. You can explore online food magazines for inspiration.

- **Options for submission:**
  - A written description
  - A multimedia description paired with images
  - A voice recording
  - A video recording
  - If you have another idea, propose it!

- **If you're stuck:**
  - Read/listen to the essay "No Woman, No Cry" as an exemplar to get inspired.
  - Close your eyes and think about what the item looks like, smells like, tastes like. Remember the place where you were when you had it. Outside, inside? Who was there? What did you see, hear, smell?
  - Draw the food first. Google the food for images and describe what you see or sketch an image with colored pencils before incorporating it into a memory.
  - Once you have the colors in mind, check out BenjaminMoore.com to find a fun way to describe the color.

This exemplar lesson on narrative writing could take many forms, but let's explore what this could look like as a whole-group rotation, as pictured in figure 3.5, where the entire class rotates between offline and online learning activities. The lesson below may span one or two class periods, depending on the length of the classes. It's important not to rush students through the parts of this lesson to ensure they have opportunities to control the pace at which they navigate the various learning activities.

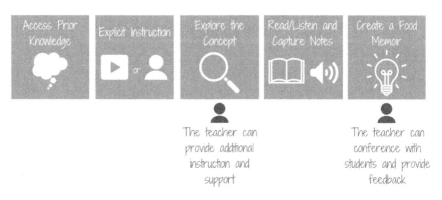

Figure 3.5: Whole Group Rotation Lesson for Narrative Writing

OFFLINE: ACCESS PRIOR KNOWLEDGE ACTIVITY. The teacher can begin the lesson by asking students to access and share their prior knowledge. What comes to mind when they hear the word *imagery*? What do they think they know about imagery? Where did this prior knowledge come from (e.g., another class, a book, a conversation with a family member)? Teachers can invite students to share their prior knowledge in one of two ways: a) spend five minutes writing in response to a prompt or b) engage in a small-group discussion with their peers.

OFFLINE OR ONLINE: EXPLICIT INSTRUCTION. The teacher has two options for explicit instruction in class. He can use a mini-lesson format to explain what imagery and descriptive details are, how to identify them, and what their purpose is in a text. He can also record a short video to introduce this concept to the class. To maximize student agency, he could allow students the option to select the mode of instruction they think will be most accessible and effective for them. Even teachers who plan to present a concept live may want to consider the benefit of creating a companion video to give students an option to decide which mode will work best for them. The video provides a resource students can access for support or repeat instruction after the live session is over.

Initially, we realize the knee-jerk response to this suggestion may be that teachers feel they are doing double the work, but video content pays dividends by saving teachers time because they do not have to repeat explanations and models.

ONLINE: EXPLORE THE CONCEPT. After students have had the opportunity to hear explicit instruction on imagery, they select a method for further exploration. They can choose to watch a video on imagery, review the textbook section on imagery, or work in collaborative groups to complete an online scavenger hunt to find their own examples of imagery. This self-paced exploration invites students to build on their understanding of this concept individually or collaboratively.

OFFLINE: READ/LISTEN AND CAPTURE NOTES. Students read and/or listen to "No Woman, No Cry." As students self-pace through the reading on their own, listen to an audio track as they read, or take turns reading with a partner, they will capture their notes. Teachers can provide agency here as well, inviting students to highlight examples of imagery in the passage, annotate the text, or fill in a graphic organizer.

As students read and capture their notes, teachers can work with students who need additional support. They can guide the reading and note-taking process by pulling an individual learner or a small group of students into a teacher-led reading and note-taking session.

OFFLINE OR ONLINE: CREATE A FOOD MEMOIR USING IMAGERY. Students can select the way in which they want to express and communicate their food memoir. Students may choose to complete a written description, create a multimedia description that pairs text with images, or record a podcast or video mimicking a cooking channel show. If students have another idea, they are welcome to propose it.

As students work to create their food memoir, the teacher can pull individual students for conferencing sessions focused on discussing the student's progress toward goals or providing focused, actionable feedback on a draft of their memoir.

Here is another example of a lesson in elementary math, using materials from Engage NY/Eureka.[8] This example demonstrates how you can use an adopted curriculum and give it the UDL/BL treatment, which will ensure that students have options and choices in their learning and that you are freed up to provide differentiated instruction based on formative assessment data.

ELEMENTARY MATH

GOAL

- Demonstrate the possible whole-number side lengths of rectangles with areas of 24, 36, 48, or 72 square units using the associative property. UDL tip: Always post lesson goals and target success criteria.

METHODS

- **Must do:** Complete fluency activity.

- **Options:** Provide an option for students to participate in one of the fluency activities outlined in the Eureka lesson. Create stations with directions on all four activities. Encourage students to choose the activity that will challenge and engage them.

- **Must do:**
  - Diagnostic assessment: Application problem.

- **Options:** Choose one of the following problems.
  - Problem A: The banquet table in a restaurant measures 3 feet by 6 feet. For a large party, workers at the restaurant place 2 banquet tables side by side to create 1 long table. Find the area of the new, longer table.
  - Problem B: One-fourth of the banquet table has an area of 9 square feet. If the width of the table is 3 feet, what is the length? What is the area of the table?
- **Must do:** Provide explicit instruction for learners on 36 square units using the Eureka lesson. Next provide the following options to continue with 24, 48, and 72 square units.
- **Options:**
  - Stay with teacher in small group
  - Watch recording of Grade 3.4, Lesson 11 with Duane Habecker, who creates mini-lessons on YouTube for every Eureka[9] lesson. The video can be paused, rewound, and replayed for those who need repeated viewing of the concept. Note: The Edpuzzle platform allows educators to extend the work of a video by placing multiple-choice and open-ended questions at strategic points throughout the video to encourage students to think critically about the information presented and provide the teacher with formative assessment data.
  - Use the Zearn website (zearn.org) to review and extend the work of the lesson. Zearn is a free website that mirrors the Eureka lessons.

MATERIALS
- Ensure that the following materials are available:
  - Manipulatives
  - Whiteboards
  - Number lines
  - Deconstructed examples

ASSESSMENTS
- **Must do:** Complete the Eureka problem set.
- **Options:**
  - Complete on paper or on Edulastic
  - Provide extension activities for when students finish, including the following options:
    - Go back to fluency activities

- An Open Middle (openmiddle.com) problem. UDL tip: Provide challenge options that delve deeper into mathematical concepts and create connections across domains
- A math fact fluency game/activity
- **Must do:** Student debrief.
- **Options:** At the end of the lesson, allow students to participate in the debrief by reflecting in writing, on Seesaw, or by chatting with a partner or small group regarding one of the following questions:
  - How did the Application Problem connect to today's lesson?
  - How did the Fluency Practice help prepare you for the lesson?

CHOOSE YOUR PATH HYPERDOC/MINI-PLAYLIST. Let's explore what the math lesson above might look like as a lesson using a hyperdoc or mini-playlist format. Unlike a traditional lesson that requires students to move through each step, solving the same problems, this lesson lends itself to students making key decisions throughout the process. Essentially, there are five parts of the lesson: a) the anticipatory set with the fluency activities, b) diagnostic assessment, c) explicit instruction, d) application, and e) reflection.

Imagine a teacher built this lesson in a digital slide deck. The first slide in this choose-your-math path would invite the students to decide which of the fluency activities taken from the Eureka math lesson they want to tackle. *Which fluency activity feels like the best fit? Which activity sounds most engaging?* This gives students the agency to choose which activity they want to engage with and allows them to self-differentiate, choosing a challenge that is within their ability to be successful.

Once students complete the fluency activity, the next slide is a "would you rather" with the two diagnostic assessment problems. Students decide which problem they want to spend time working on and document their work, inserting an image into the slide.

The third slide provides three options for explicit instruction. Students can work directly with the teacher, complete an Edpuzzle lesson self-pacing through a video explanation paired with questions, or they can use the Zearn website to review concepts. Teachers can make a range of materials available to complement both instruction and application, including manipulatives, whiteboards, number lines, and deconstructed examples.

After students complete the activity of their choice on the explicit instruction slide, they move onto slide four, which targets practice and application. Again, they have a "would you rather" choice. They can complete a problem set on paper or on Edulastic. They can also access extension activities for when students finish, such as additional fluency activities, an Open Middle problem, or math fact fluency game or activity.

Finally, they move onto the fifth and final slide for their reflection. Students can reflect on the lesson in writing, in a video recording, or by debriefing with classmates in a discussion. This is also an opportunity to collect feedback from students about their experience with the choose-your-path hyperdoc/mini-playlist format. As teachers try new approaches, it is always a good practice to check in with students to see how it went from their perspective.

As you can see from the examples above, UDL and blended learning can be applied to curriculum you design yourself, and help you transform an adopted curriculum into a more equitable, more inclusive learning experience that frees you to provide differentiated support to flexible groups of learners. In both the narrative writing and elementary math lesson, all students have access to grade-level instruction and also have the opportunity to build expert learning skills, self-differentiate their learning, and receive the targeted intervention or enrichment necessary for success.

SUMMARIZE, REFLECT, AND DISCUSS

Our design work is a reflection of what we value. If we celebrate student variability as a strength, then we must design learning experiences that reflect the diversity of skills, interests, needs, and preferences that exist in a class. A one-size-fits-all approach ignores the diversity in our classrooms. Committing to proactively designing goals, methods, materials, and assessments is critical to ensuring there are flexible pathways for students to achieve and engage with learning experiences that matter.

- How does the shoe store analogy help you to better appreciate the importance of variability and flexibility in design work?
- As an educator and designer, you are called to architect learning experiences for all learners by creating lessons with flexible goals, methods, materials, and assessments. As you think about your current practice, which of these areas would most benefit from using the dual lenses of UDL and blended learning?
- How will you change your learning environment to allow the time and space for mess-making, which is a critical component of design?

CHAPTER 4

Instruction:
Let's Leave Lecture Halls
in the Past

From Sit-and-Get to Active Engagement

Catlin

I experienced very different approaches to instruction, most poignantly in college.

I remember my first few weeks wandering around UCLA, trying to get my bearings. The campus was vast. So, too, were many of the lecture halls where I spent my days. In that first year, I was enrolled in the required general education courses alongside other freshmen and sophomores. My first quarter, I signed up for an odd assortment of classes—statistics, anthropology, art history, and political science. These courses checked certain boxes. They represented hoops I had to jump through before I could get to the classes I really wanted to take.

On a bright Southern California morning, I walked across campus to my first art history lecture. I pulled open the huge door and stared open-mouthed at the giant lecture hall. There was row upon row of tightly packed fold-down seats facing a large stage with a podium and white projector screen. I selected a seat at the end of a row in the middle of the room and observed the flood of students entering, many looking as bewildered as I felt.

Our professor took the stage and proceeded to spend the next hour and a half talking from the podium. He flashed the occasional image of artwork or a map onto the screen. There wasn't a single word on any of the images he projected. As he flew through information, I sat hunched over my little wood tray furiously taking notes. I had no idea how to spell any of the artists' names or the obscure cities where specific events had taken place. Instead, I tried to write down everything this professor was saying and capture phonetic spellings of people, events, and places so I could look them up immediately following this lecture.

By the end of the class, I had a dozen pages of scribbled notes. My right hand felt more like a claw, and my middle finger had a visible dent where I held my pen. The worst part of this experience was that I left the lecture hall with the sinking feeling that I didn't know any more about art history than I had ninety minutes prior. I was going to have to make sense of these notes later with the help of my textbook and a visit to my professor's office hours.

Each of my general education courses followed this same pattern. Too many students, too much information presented too fast, and not enough time to process what I was hearing, ask questions, or engage in conversation with my peers. It was frustrating, and I struggled to understand the material. I did not enjoy the majority of my general education classes those first two years of college.

My experience changed dramatically when I signed up for my upper-division courses in the English department. I remember the anticipation and nervousness I felt walking through the sculpture garden on the way to my first upper-division English class on the literary works of Jane Austin. The classroom was small, easily accommodating the seventeen students enrolled, and the chairs in the room were organized into a circle. There wasn't a podium. Instead, our professor sat in a chair just like mine in the circle.

Our professor introduced information, explained vocabulary, made connections between ideas, and unpacked complex concepts, but it was always in bite-size chunks and always followed by an invitation to ask questions. The class was grounded in discussion, and she challenged us with open-ended, thought-provoking questions. She pushed us to construct knowledge and make meaning together.

I loved going to that class. The professor was responsive, taking into consideration our needs in a given moment. She offered her insights without overpowering the discussion. If we were struggling with something, she would help us work through moments of confusion, uncertainty, or disagreement. I felt like my voice mattered in that class. I also realized for the first time that my classmates were invaluable resources. I left every class buzzing with new ideas and excited about what I had learned.

The stark difference between my passive experience in lower-division lecture halls and my active, engaged experience in my upper-division courses highlights the different approaches that teachers can take when providing instruction, regardless of whether a class is happening in person, online, or via a combination of the two.

One problem with a lecture-style approach to transferring information is that the capacity of the brain's working memory is small.[1] Inundating students with large quantities of new information at one time is ineffective generally. Instead, students are more likely to retain information that is presented in small chunks. Students also need opportunities to mentally engage with the information. Most teachers know that lectures are unlikely to maintain student interest and acknowledge the limitations of a whole-group, one-size-fits-all format. Yet, whole-group instruction remains a dominant approach because of the massive amounts of information teachers are expected to cover in a school year. It begs the question, what is the point of racing through curriculum if students do not understand it?

Unpacking Instruction

Instruction is one of the teacher's primary roles and responsibilities. A teacher must explain complex concepts, teach vocabulary, model strategies, and aid comprehension. Yet, instruction can take many forms. It can serve to relegate students to a passive, consumptive role, or it can engage students' higher-order thinking skills and encourage members of a class community to make meaning together. One type of instruction is static and the other is dynamic.

In the book *Explicit Instruction: Effective and Efficient Teaching*,[2] the authors note, "Terminology aside, perhaps the most basic question in education is this: 'What is the best way to teach students?' First, we believe that there is no one best way to teach. Instruction should be based on students' needs."

Both UDL and blended learning support self-directed learning and instruction based on student needs. It's important to note that self-directed learning doesn't mean that a teacher doesn't provide framing or direct instruction to students. Research is clear that self-directed learning may be (a) student-directed, (b) student-and teacher-directed, or (c) teacher-directed.[3]

In this book, we discuss self-directed learning as student-and teacher-directed. Making meaning is a partnership and happens in a combination of whole-group, small-group, and individualized instruction.

Explicit instruction is characterized by a series of supports or scaffolds, where students are guided through the learning process with clear statements about the purpose and rationale for learning, clear explanations and demonstrations of the instructional goal and expected outcomes, and supported practice with feedback until independent mastery has been achieved.[4]

We have worked with countless educators who have designed and delivered instruction using a hybrid or remote model. We know that many of these educators are frustrated by whole-class video-conference lessons because they feel like they are wasting forty-five minutes instructing thirty kids who appear as black boxes and who are potentially AWOL.

In one particular scenario, teachers were asked to explain the value of providing forty-five minutes of whole-group instruction. Their answer: "Oh, there is no value at all. It's district policy that we have to keep them online for forty-five minutes." When asked what they thought would be more effective, the team agreed it would be valuable to start with a diagnostic assessment where students could determine the level of support they needed, and then after a short mini-lesson, they could choose to stay on to ask questions, begin to work on formative assessments, or dive more deeply into resources like prerecorded lectures, the online textbook, or collaborative groupings. After a formative assessment, the teachers wanted an opportunity to provide explicit instruction in small instructional groups based on student needs. "Yeeeeessss," we wanted to tell them. "Do all of that!"

The question, always, is how.

Asynchronous vs. Synchronous Instruction

The shift to universally designed blended learning requires that teachers consider *how* they teach in addition to what they teach. They also must consider which mode of instruction—asynchronous or synchronous—will be most effective in transferring information to a diverse group of learners.

Teachers can make instruction available asynchronously with video or provide synchronous real-time instruction in the classroom or online via videoconferencing. Teachers often ask, "When should I make a video?" Our answer is simple: "If you are going to explain the same thing the same way for everyone, make a video." Let's explore the benefits of video-based instruction.

Videos have the clear advantage of shifting control over time, place, and pace to the student. Video also allows students to manipulate the information in ways that are not possible during live instruction. They can pause a video, rewind it, or rewatch it as many times as they need. Students can adjust the speed of a video or read closed captions, making the content more accessible. One important accessibility consideration for video is that the mode is largely visual. Ensuring that there is a clear auditory component is important for students who may have a visual impairment or who may struggle with visual comprehension.[5] However, video can be incredibly flexible and provide numerous opportunities for students to personalize their experience.

Video can be used to capture the following if teachers plan to provide the same explanation to all students.

- short lectures (emphasis on the word *short*)
- mini-lessons
- modeling a strategy
- demonstrating a process
- directions for a multistep assignment or task

Video content can replace whole-group instruction if the entire class needs to hear the same foundational explanation or see the same model. Since students process information at different rates, it's advantageous for them to have more control over the experience.

Teachers are always curious about the optimal length of video instruction. There was an empirical study published that measured student engagement while watching video content in massive online open-source courses (MOOCs).[6] Since MOOCs are composed largely of adult learners, K-12 educators have to take the results with a grain of salt, but the findings suggested that student engagement peaked at the six-minute mark. There was a subtle decline between six and nine minutes and a much more dramatic decrease after the nine-minute mark. So, there could be a case to make that six minutes is the sweet spot for video content.

As a rule of thumb, we recommend one minute of video content per year in school. If a third-grade teacher wants to present information in a video, we suggest three or four minutes of video content. A ninth-grade teacher would aim for nine-to-ten-minute videos.

The trick to making short yet effective videos is to chunk information and keep it simple. To begin, select a single topic, concept, or objective to be the focus of a video. Narrowing the focus will prevent you from trying to cover too much ground in a single video. It is better to create a couple of short videos as opposed to one longer video. In fact, the study of student engagement with videos found that "video length was by far the most significant indicator of engagement."[7] It's also key not to overwhelm the learner's cognitive load with irrelevant visuals, unnecessary information, or busy backgrounds.[8]

Another strategy you can use to maximize the impact of a video is to wrap it in a more complete learning experience. To do this, plan video instruction in three parts: a) pre-video activity, b) engagement around video content, and c) post-video activity, as pictured in figure 4.1.

**Figure 4.1: Three-Part Approach to Flipping
Instruction with Video**

Instead of simply asking students to watch a video and take notes, how can we pique their interest, drive inquiry, or assess prior knowledge *before* they watch a video? Designing a pre-video activity creates context for the instruction or model that students will be watching. This pre-video activity can provide you and the students with helpful formative assessment data about where each student is beginning in terms of their prior knowledge.

As students watch a video, they need to be prompted to think about what they are seeing so they do not slip into a passive, consumptive role. Wrapping a video in a lesson using software that periodically asks students questions about the content encourages them to think more deeply about the information, which will, in turn, make the video lesson more effective. To implement UDL, pair a video with a guided note template or an online discussion prompt that asks students to identify and discuss the information presented using multiple means of expression. For example, students would be encouraged to reflect on a question and answer it in writing, by drawing a model, or by recording a short video.

Finally, the video lesson should be followed by a post-video activity that encourages students to take what they just learned and *do* something with it. It is during this "extend and apply" work that students are likely to hit bumps and need additional support, scaffolding, reteaching, guided practice, or feedback. This work extending and applying is ideal for synchronous class time, so students benefit from the support of a subject-area expert and a community of peers. Videos are a useful vehicle for shifting some of the explanation and instruction online so that teachers can create flexible groups and provide differentiated, hands-on work.

Video, UDL, and Blended Learning in Action

Imagine you are designing a lesson in which students have to write an argument about the content under study. In order to help them articulate their claim, it's important that you provide instruction on how to write a clear and concise thesis statement. It would be effective to record a short video introducing thesis statements where you explain what a thesis statement is, where it belongs in a response, and what elements need to be included in it. That foundational explanation is important for all students to hear. Since you need to provide the same explanation for everyone, recording a short five-minute video would be more effective than providing that explanation live when students would have only one chance to "get it." However, when it comes to drafting a thesis statement, we can predict that students will need different levels of support.

One group of students might benefit from seeing you model the process of constructing a thesis statement. To provide this model, you can conduct a think-aloud, making your thought process explicit as you write a thesis for another prompt. Another group of students might need to see a model *and* work with a thesis statement sentence frame that provides them with a structure for organizing the information.

Unfortunately, when we dedicate significant amounts of class time to a basic explanation of the *how* for the entire class, there often isn't time to think about the supports and scaffolds that individuals or groups of students may need to successfully implement a strategy or apply a skill. It is this differentiated and personalized approach to instruction that will be most effective in helping students make individual progress toward understanding key concepts and mastering specific skills.

Because synchronous instruction, like all synchronous learning, should be engaging, differentiated, and prioritize human interaction, consider pulling the following into real-time instruction:

- interactive modeling sessions
- guided practice and application
- reteaching
- real-time feedback and coaching
- inquiry and discussion

The key to making the most of synchronous instruction is to bring your design-thinking eye to the process of structuring this precious time with students. What is the objective of this time? Are you focusing on a specific concept, standard, or skill? How can you best support students in understanding this concept or mastering this skill?

There are many ways to structure a synchronous session, but the first question to ask yourself is, "What grouping strategy makes the most sense given the purpose of our time together?" Early in the pandemic, many teachers were using whole-group sessions without much success. A whole-group session online using videoconferencing software is even more challenging given that so many students do not turn on their cameras and choose not to actively engage in those sessions. As you plan, identify the purpose of your time with students and select the grouping strategy that makes the most sense, as pictured in table 4.1.

Grouping Strategy	Purpose
Whole-group sessions	Circle time or "welcome to the week" meeting Start-of-the-week routines (e.g., student of the week, class calendar, birthday shoutouts) Community-building activities Overview of the week • What will be covered? Is there an essential question guiding the work this week? • Are there large-scale assignments or projects students will be working on? • Are there any organizational tips or reminders that students need to be successful?
Small-group sessions	Differentiated instruction • Use formative assessment data to flexibly group students and provide the necessary instruction, supports, and scaffold for each group Engage all students • Capitalize on the smaller group dynamic to engage every student in the activities or discussion Collect formative assessment data • Listen and observe as students chat, problem-solve, or apply what they are learning • Ask students to answer quick poll questions or complete a quick assessment (e.g., quiz or short written response) to gauge the effectiveness of a session
Individual sessions	Personalized instruction • Use this time to meet individual learners' needs • Reteach • Provide additional supports, scaffolds, acceleration, or enrichment • Conduct more think-alouds and modeling sessions

	Guide practice • Conference about progress • Use the student's goal-setting sheet to anchor these conversations and identify what students need to continue making progress • Real-time feedback or assessment sessions • Give students focused, actionable feedback on a piece of work in progress • Conduct a think-aloud assessing student work so they understand their assessment scores

Table 4.1: Grouping Students for a Specific Purpose

When we suggest that teachers consider small-group instruction, they often ask, "What are the other students doing while I'm working with the small group?" This question seems to imply that students cannot do meaningful work unless a teacher is directing and monitoring the learning. We want to challenge that assumption. Students, even young learners and learners with complex support needs, benefit from opportunities to direct their own learning. They need to enjoy a degree of autonomy and agency in the learning process.

Watch Me Work Night

Catlin

I remember when my own children were toddlers and attended a Montessori day school. Every three months they hosted a Watch Me Work Night. The kids would give us a tour around the classroom and show off their favorite works. I both loathed and loved these evenings. As a working mother with two young children, the last thing I wanted to do after a long day of teaching was pack up my kids and head back to their school. I was exhausted and had a to-do list a mile long, but I also loved seeing my children light up with excitement and pride as they showed off their classroom and shared their favorite activities.

They showed me the intricate puzzles they assembled, the sound books they labored over with crayons, and the magnetic building blocks they used to construct elaborate structures born from their imaginations. Each time I attended a Watch Me Work Night and observed my children take one work item off the shelf at a time (that was the rule), explain its purpose and show me how it worked, then put it back with care, I was filled with admiration for these teachers who had taught my children how to navigate this learning space with so much respect.

I think of those Watch Me Work Nights each time an educator expresses skepticism about the students' ability to manage their own behavior or lead the learning in a classroom. These behaviors and skills must be taught, and every student is capable of learning without a teacher orchestrating the process.

Brain as Learning Machine

In a podcast interview, Zaretta Hammond, author of *Culturally Responsive Teaching and the Brain*, makes the point that the human brain is wired to learn. Hammond says, "The brain is a learning machine. It does not need to go to school to learn."[9] That's an important point to remember. We can architect learning experiences to aid learning and the development of specific skills, but students do not actually *need* us to learn. They are capable learners on their own.

Once we embrace the reality that students can, in fact, learn without us monitoring every aspect of their experience, we benefit from exploring models that allow us to design lessons that create the space necessary to work with small groups of students. Our favorite blended learning model to achieve this small-group dynamic is the station rotation model. It is flexible enough to work in class or online. Essentially, the teacher breaks the class into groups. The total number of groups may depend on the variety of needs in a classroom, the ideal size of the groups, or the amount of time a teacher has for a given class.

For the sake of simplicity, let's imagine you are designing a lesson for a sixty-minute class period. Divide the class into three groups and rotate each group through three stations. Remember, these "stations" do not need to denote a physical location in a classroom since some classes may not meet in person. Instead, you can think of them as discrete learning activities. Each group will spend approximately twenty minutes at each station: 1) teacher-led station, 2) online station, 3) offline station. The teacher-led station presents the perfect opportunity to provide explicit, engaging, and differentiated instruction. There are several different strategies a teacher can use to structure this time with students. Below are a few strategies for structuring a teacher-led station to ensure the experience is engaging and student-centered.

HOOK THE GROUP. This strategy inverts the traditional approach to instruction. Instead of leading with the explanation or modeling, the teacher begins by presenting students with an unfamiliar problem, question, task, or challenge. Then the group must work together to figure out how to solve the problem, answer the question, or tackle the new task or challenge. This requires critical thinking, communication, collaboration, and creativity—the four Cs of twenty-first-century learning! It also demands that students get comfortable in a space of productive struggle. They do not have the option to throw their hands in the air and say, "We don't know how to do this." The goal is to figure it out. What strategies have they used in the past that might work in this situation? What questions or wonderings do they have that might help the group make sense of this? What resources do they have at their disposal that might help them?

As students wrestle with the task, focus your energy on listening and observing. It's amazing how much we learn from simply watching students at work. Observation yields powerful formative assessment data. This is an aspect of teaching that educators miss when working exclusively online; however, this can still be achieved in a videoconference session if we create space for students to work together and engage in conversations around shared tasks. Bouncing in and out of breakout rooms and observing students working on a task can help us to identify misconceptions, gaps in knowledge, and areas of strength.

Once the students have had time to work together, pull them back together for a debrief. What strategies did they use? What bumps did they hit? How did they work together to figure out how to approach this unfamiliar challenge? What questions do they have?

Finally, end with instruction and modeling. The effect of following the hook activity with the explanation is fascinating. Students lean into the instruction. They are curious because they have sat in a space of productive struggle and *want* to know how to solve the problem, answer the question, or complete the task. This is what we want!

I DO, WE DO, GROUPS DO, YOU DO. The direct instruction model is a great way to support students in learning a new skill or working through a new process. This approach to structuring a teacher-led station begins with the teacher explaining and modeling so students know what they are working toward.

After a demonstration, guide the group through a "we do," where the group works through another similar task together. Ask students to share their suggestions and guide them as they work through this second example. In class, it is easy to call on students and ask them to contribute their ideas. Online you may struggle with the "we do," fearing the chaos that might ensue if multiple students are unmuting at once. However, there are ways to make this work more seamlessly: simply asking specific students to unmute and share, encouraging students to put their suggestions in the chat, or asking students to post them in a shared digital space that is visible to the group. It's important that we not neglect opportunities to engage students online, even if the process isn't as smooth as it would be in a classroom.

A "groups do" allows for a more gradual release and encourages students to collaborate in order to work through another example without any teacher support. In the classroom, you can strategically pair students or break the group into smaller groups to work through another example. Just as with the hook-the-group strategy, you can provide tasks at different levels of rigor to ensure all students can be successful. For example, if students are working on a specific type of math problem or attempting to make inferences about a text, the problem or text they work with may be at slightly different levels of academic rigor. As pairs or groups of students work together, this is another opportunity for the teacher to watch, listen, and identify students who may need additional support before transitioning to the "you do" for independent practice.

During the "you do," students attempt to work on their own, taking what they learned in the previous stages and applying it without teacher or peer support. In this stage, project a timer and give students time in class or online to work through the "you do" task. For those students learning online, it is critical that this time be built into the videoconference session. That way, if students get stuck or need additional support, you can pull a student into a breakout room to provide additional instruction and work through another example together. This helps students working online feel seen and supported.

PRESENT, PAUSE, DISCUSS (REPEAT). If you are going to use their teacher-led station to transfer information, make that experience interactive and engaging by using a present-pause-discuss strategy to structure the experience. Begin by chunking the content you want to "present," and limit the presentation of new information to five-minute segments. Remember, students can only take in a limited amount of new information at a time, so we do not want to overwhelm them by presenting too much at one time. Create a visual presentation that has keywords, vocabulary terms, and facts paired with relevant media. This will help students who struggle to process information presented verbally. The pairing of the verbal explanation with a visual will help more students to be successful and provides multiple means of representation.

After you have presented a chunk of new information, remember to pause. During the "pause," students have time to fill in their notes. The style of note-taking is an opportunity for meaningful choice. Some students may prefer more traditional Cornell-style notes, while others may enjoy a more artistic approach with sketchnotes. Ask students to review their notes to identify and share the most important points. You can also request that each student write a question they have about the information that was presented.

During the "discuss" section, use the main points and questions generated by the group to engage them in an informal conversation to ensure that everyone understands the information that was presented before you move on to the next chunk. As students get used to this approach, they gain confidence engaging with new information and articulating areas of confusion. Instead of being passive receivers of this new information, they realize that it is their responsibility to think critically about the information being presented. When you use this approach to instruction, it normalizes the process of asking questions, identifying areas of confusion, and engaging in conversation that can help students to achieve deeper levels of understanding.

SUMMARIZE, REFLECT, AND DISCUSS

Universal Design for Learning (UDL) and blended learning encourage teachers to design flexible opportunities for students to self-differentiate their learning while supplementing explicit instruction using flexible groupings. In addition to clarifying vocabulary; highlighting patterns, critical ideas, and relationships; and guiding information processing, instruction should create opportunities for connection. Instead of positioning the teacher as the expert at the front of the room, explicit instruction can be used to support expert learning, develop the teacher-student relationship, and increase student engagement. To do this effectively, teachers need to be strategic and intentional about how they use asynchronous and synchronous instruction to help students make progress toward learning objectives.

- When universally designing blended learning experiences, you can build expert learning while also building relationships and targeted instruction through a model that is student-and teacher-directed. Which aspects of your model are currently teacher-directed that you recognize you can transition to being student-directed?

- Having time with small groups of students and individual students is critical to building relationships and offering targeted instruction and support to supplement universally designed learning opportunities. How could you create a model in your own learning environment that allows you to have this time with the whole group, small groups, and individuals?

- Reflect on the example of how to facilitate blended learning within a station model where each group will spend approximately twenty minutes at each station: 1) teacher-led station, 2) online station, 3) offline station. What types of activities, in your content area, would be suited for each station?

CHAPTER 5

Facilitator:
Channel Your Inner Pigeon Fancier

Waiting for Benny

Katie

In Groton, Massachusetts, there are no pigeons. Especially not in our yard. This is important to remember because the events that follow happened because the presence of a pigeon in our yard was so incredibly novel. I first noticed the pigeon when I looked out the window and saw two neighbors huddled down near my front yard, pointing at the pigeon with as much awe as if there were an ostrich hanging out on the end of the cul de sac. I couldn't see the pigeon, but I saw their expressions so I went outside to join them. The pigeon, a plump little bird, hopped around the yard like a bunny.

"Can you believe it?" my neighbor asked. "A pigeon."

If you live in an area where the pigeon population rivals humans, you may think we are mad. But this pigeon was special. My home office faces the front yard, so throughout the day, my kids made regular visits to the pigeon, and bikers and walkers stopped to check on the bird. My daughter, Aylin, a lover of all sentient beings, tried to lure the pigeon to her with hamster food and peanuts.

Around 4:00 p.m. that evening, our phones started pinging with an emergency alert. Microbursts, or small tornados, were in the area, which meant we needed to hide in the basement. Our home abuts a conservation area, and pine trees close to a hundred feet tall loom above our house. "Get away from the windows," my husband urged, but one question loomed.

"But Mom, what about the pigeon?"

We debated the danger of playing footsie with Mother Nature to bring the pigeon to safety, but my husband, Lon, was having none of that. We would leave the pigeon. The microbursts took down a tree and our patio set but spared the bird.

As soon as we were able, the kids rushed outside to check on the small, wet bird. My son, Brecan, said, "Mom, don't you feel bad for its owner?"

"Brec, why on earth would you say that the bird has an owner? There are billions of pigeons in the world."

He looked at me like I was dense and said, "Umm, because it's wearing tags." Now, as a pet owner myself, I knew what I had to do. I had to capture the pigeon. Imagine the show the neighbors got as I ran around the yard in bare feet with a pillowcase trying to save the sweet bird. When victory was mine, we set up the dog crate and made him comfortable with a bowl of water and a handful of hamster food. While he lapped/pecked at the water, I examined the tags. To my dismay, the only information on the tags read, *IF ROX 025*. Clearly not as helpful as a dog tag, but as an expert learner, I had something to work with.

Turns out, if you search "pigeon tag IF" in Google, your first hit will be the lost and found page of the International Federation of American Homing Pigeon Fanciers, Inc. Bingo.

ROX was a code for the coop, Roxbury Lofts, in Roxbury, a neighborhood in Boston. Lucky me, there was a name and phone number. And this is how I met Rafael Bachier. I called Rafael, a wonderful, kind man, while he was at work and sputtered, "I have your pigeon."

"What? Which one?"

I looked at the bird, still drinking from the bowl, and guessed, "Umm . . . 025?"

"Benny," he exclaimed. "You have Benny!"

Later that evening, Rafael drove forty-seven miles to Groton to pick up Benny, an elite racing pigeon who clocks 70 mph! Little Benny was only six weeks old and had never flown more than a mile before his trek to my front yard. Rafael guessed that he was chased off by a hawk, and by the time he landed in front of my house, he was too exhausted to go anywhere else. He picked up the bird expertly, checking under the wings, and held him close like a kitten.

And then he dropped the bomb on us. Apparently, Benny was at a critical homing stage, and he may have imprinted on our home. "If he comes back," Rafael laughed, "he's your pigeon." Enough time has passed where I think that Benny is safely homed to the Roxbury Coops, but my interest in pigeon racing is still going strong.

That night, Rafael taught me a lot about pigeon racing. The American Racing Pigeon Union has ten thousand members and oversees eight hundred local clubs; another several hundred clubs are affiliated with the International Federation of American Homing Pigeon Fanciers.

Pigeon fanciers are not just pet owners but generals of a sky army and athletic trainers.[1] They are committed to ensuring that their flock can meet its goal: to find home. To do this, they hand-feed each pigeon to establish trust. Each day, they awake before dawn, before it's too hot for flying, to drive the birds farther and farther away to build their endurance. Supporting these birds makes fanciers quite the facilitators. But the training pays off. Thousands of pigeons can be released thousands of miles from home, and they will all make their way back to where they started. How lovely to think of us preparing students to go out on their own to reach their goals. It begins with facilitating learning, as opposed to directing learning.

Core Tasks for Facilitation

Facilitation is arguably the most important role we have as educators in a flexible learning landscape. Our work facilitating learning is how students feel seen and supported, whether they are in a classroom, online, or working in a combination of the two. In the previous chapter, we discuss the importance of instruction and continually note how crucial it is that students learn together in a group. Fostering expert learning in our learning environments requires that we build our skills in facilitating students' learning regardless of the learning environment. Think of facilitation as a part of instruction, but it is important enough that we want to dedicate a chapter to how we can facilitate learning so it is a valuable part of instruction. Research identifies three "core tasks" for facilitation: promoting participation, ensuring equity, and building trust.[2] These core tasks need to be present in both the pigeon community and in our classrooms.

PROMOTING PARTICIPATION. Promoting participation is critical for student engagement. As a facilitator of learning, there are numerous techniques you can employ to ensure that all learners have equal opportunities to participate in the learning process in ways that are relevant, authentic, and meaningful. In UDL, it is critical that students have options and choices for participation. Traditional approaches to participation are generally teacher-directed and conducive to students assuming a passive role and a general reluctance to participate in class.

One common technique is "Initiate, Respond, Evaluate." In this approach, you pose a question, call on a student to answer (either voluntarily or involuntarily), and then evaluate the response and offer feedback. This technique can result in a game of gotcha, where we check in to see if students are paying attention. One way is to write student names down on popsicle sticks, and when you pose a question, choose a popsicle stick and ask the student to answer. Clearly, there are considerable issues with this technique. One of which, of course, is that the student picked might not have an answer. Another is that only a single student can participate at any given time. In order to facilitate meaningful participation, we have to design opportunities for all students to participate.

One technique to consider is "Google or Doodle." Before posting a question, set a timer for five minutes for learners to review their notes, research the question online, sketch out an answer, create a concept map, or collaborate with classmates to define an answer. By providing options to foster collaboration, activate background knowledge, and refer to resources, you give all students opportunities to build knowledge and craft an answer, which makes "Initiate, Respond, Evaluate" much more meaningful.

Another oldie but goodie for facilitating class participation is the group discussion. We all know that these can go south quickly. Predictable barriers include students socializing off-task, a couple of students monopolizing the conversation, and/or students who struggle with social expectations or demands. When we can identify barriers, we can design pathways to minimize them. The UDL Guidelines remind educators to co-create clear expectations for group work (e.g., rubrics, norms, etc.), to cultivate communities of learners engaged in common interests or activities, and to use flexible rather than fixed grouping.

ENSURING EQUITY. An effective facilitator of learning recognizes that strategic thinking and careful planning are critical to provide students with equal opportunities to learn, participate in meaningful ways, and express what they know.

In order to ensure equitable outcomes, we have to design learning opportunities with the scaffolds and supports and challenges that some students will need to be successful, and then provide them as options to all learners. And we have to recognize that providing these supports is, by definition, fair.

Some educators struggle with providing students with scaffolds like additional time, opportunities for revision, exemplars, and word banks because the one-size-fits-all system has convinced us that students should be successful without these supports. Remembering that what is necessary for some learners is good for them all will help create opportunities where learners can reflect, make choices, and use the tools that allow them to succeed in an equitable way.

BUILDING TRUST. In a universally designed classroom, students have numerous opportunities for choice and voice. When we put learners in the driver's seat, empower them to make decisions about their learning, and invite them to share feedback about our learning design, we are asking them to take risks. To facilitate effective learning, our students have to trust that we have created an environment where they can take risks, try new things, and ask for the support they need without judgment or fear.

First, as we shared throughout this text, we need to get to know our learners well to serve them authentically. In order to build trust, the class must be designed so educators can work individually and with small groups of students. Having time to work with students individually, or in small groups, is critical to building trust and facilitating learning. In a study of student-teacher trust in urban high schools, researchers learned, "Students believed teachers who 'took the time,' 'spent time with me' and 'got on me' about academic effort and performance were worth speaking to" and trusting.[3]

In addition to building relationships with students and working with them in small groups, we have to examine our practices to identify which ones may erode trust. For example, many schools embrace the concept of growth mindset. And yet . . . in these same schools teachers may deduct points for late and revised work and do not offer retakes on tests. These practices don't align with growth mindset. We expect students to try new things and take risks and then penalize them when they don't get it right, when it takes them longer than expected, or when they want to try again. We all have practices like this—ones that erode trust with our students. But when we are facilitating learning effectively, we provide spaces for students to highlight these barriers, share their feedback, and note how the learning environment could be designed differently.

Note that building trust is not just about students trusting us. If we are to facilitate expert learning, we have to trust that students can and will learn if they are given opportunities to make choices, reflect on those choices, and try again. The reluctance of educators to trust students leads to the unraveling of the learning community since students recognize they are not in control and are not active decision-makers or partners in learning.[4]

Facilitation requires us to go beyond design, to deliver a curriculum that empowers students to learn. We have an incredible opportunity to facilitate that learning through the principles of Universal Design, as we create spaces for participation; optimize choice, voice, and autonomy; and work to build trust in student autonomy.

Coaches and Learning Partners

Catlin

I compare our work facilitating learning to that of a coach. Growing up, I had a lot of coaches. I played soccer and ran track from elementary school through high school. My coaches varied in quality throughout the years. Some coaches were aggressive and yelled a lot, while others never made the effort to personally connect with me as a player. It wasn't until I decided to try out for the cross-country team my freshman year of high school that I realized how influential a coach could be.

I tried out with one objective in mind: I wanted to stay in shape for the sports I *really* cared about—soccer and track. A couple of the girls on my club soccer team ran cross-country, and they were in great shape. They never seemed to tire in games. So, I figured, *What the heck? I'll try out. If I make it, great. If not, no big deal.*

There were not that many students at tryouts. Cross-country wasn't a high-profile sport at my high school, like football or soccer. When the rosters for varsity and junior varsity were posted, I was stunned to see my name on the varsity list. The team had seven runners. I found out on the first day of practice that all seven members of the team would run in the races each week, but only the first five runners on the team would "score." Apparently, the other two runners would not officially count toward the score, but they had the important job of displacing runners on the other team. Even though I was not passionate about cross-country, the type-A, competitive, oldest child in me wanted to be one of the five runners to score.

The first week of practice, I began to question my decision. Even though I had years of experience running track, I was a sprinter. I ran the 100, 4 x 100, 200, and 400. The 400-meter—one lap around the track—was my least favorite because it required the most stamina and always left me feeling nauseous. Well, every day at cross-country felt like that. I started to think I had made a huge mistake.

My coach is the only reason I did not quit. He was the first coach I had ever had who made time to meet one-on-one with me to talk about my goals. Why was I running cross-country? What did I want to accomplish? I was honest. I told him, "I want to be a strong enough runner to score, but I am really doing this to get into great shape for my other sports." He didn't make me feel bad for admitting that I wasn't a passionate cross-country runner; instead he used what I cared about—competition and conditioning—to motivate me.

He knew that I had zero training as a long-distance runner. He would pull the team together at the start of practice to provide instruction and model technique for the group. Then, when we were out on conditioning runs, he would often run alongside me, suggesting small adjustments to my form. This personalized feedback on my specific strengths and weaknesses helped me develop a better understanding of myself as a runner. He showed me how to adjust my form to release the tension in my upper body to avoid cramping. He talked to me about how my foot was hitting the ground and explained how running long distances required that I use a different approach. He spent time explaining why something was important, how to do it, and what the impact on my performance would be. Then he would patiently provide reminders until my form improved.

At our Friday practice in the third week of the season, our coach announced that he was adding a Sunday run to our schedule. Our team would meet in the morning and run Cheeseboro Canyon Trail in the hills of Agoura, California. The trail was 10.4 miles. My jaw dropped. I could barely run the 3.5 miles required by most races!

I blurted out, "I can't run that far."

My coach responded calmly, "I don't want to hear 'I can't' statements, Catlin. You can do exactly what you set your mind to."

I knew when to shut my mouth and nod, but I thought his confidence in my abilities was unfounded. As I pulled on my sweatshirt and gathered my belongings at the end of practice, my coach approached me. *Crap. I'm in trouble.*

He told me Cheeseboro Canyon Trail was beautiful, it would give our bodies a break from running on pavement, and the challenge of the run would be a good bonding experience for the team.

He said, "What's the worst thing that can happen? You might have to walk part of the trail? All I'm asking is that you come with an 'I can' attitude."

I arrived at Cheeseboro at nine o'clock in the morning. The trail was lined with wildflowers and oak trees. As we started the run, I remember thinking, *I can, I can, I can.* I felt a little ridiculous, but that mantra helped as we approached the four-mile mark and I got my first side cramp. By mile six, I had hit my stride and got the elusive "second wind." There were moments when I considered walking, but my competitive nature would not allow me to stop when the rest of my team was running. The sense of accomplishment I felt as we rounded the final turn and I caught a glimpse of the parking lot was unlike anything I had ever experienced in soccer or track. I had done something I honestly did not think I was capable of doing. My coach had known I could do it, but until completing the run, I had not believed in myself. From that moment on, I trusted my cross-country coach implicitly.

Embracing Our Role as Coaches in the Classroom

As I work with teachers supporting students in blended learning environments, I want them to think about coaching kids in the same way my cross-country coach worked with me. First, he made time to get to know me and understand what motivated me and helped me to set goals for myself. Second, he provided timely, focused, and actionable feedback on my form that helped me to gradually improve as a long-distance runner. Finally, he had high expectations, believed in my ability, and presented me with challenging tasks that were within the scope of my ability (even if I didn't realize I was capable of those tasks at first).

GET TO KNOW STUDENTS AND STRIVE TO UNDERSTAND WHAT MOTIVATES THEM. As much as we would like every student to be intrinsically motivated to learn, that isn't realistic. Some students will love science and be motivated to read the dense textbook and invest time and energy into writing detailed lab reports, while other students may not.

Teachers who take the time to get to know their students and understand what motivates them will have more success engaging them in class. Making time for one-on-one conversations is easier to accomplish when teachers are utilizing blended learning models to create the space to work with individual learners. For example, you can pull students aside one by one during a blended lesson or schedule virtual office hours with individual students at the start of a semester to have these conversations.

To facilitate student learning, you can design a choose-your-learning-path experience. Imagine an elementary science lesson where the goal is that all students understand how animals adapt to their environment. The lesson can be built in a digital slide deck where each slide invites students to make key decisions about their learning. First, they decide how they want to engage with this new information. Do they want to read a text, watch a video, or listen to a podcast? Next, they move to the second slide that encourages them to spend time processing and thinking deeply about what they learned. They can take notes, create a concept map, draw sketch-notes, respond to a writing prompt, or pair up with another student and discuss what they learned. Then, they can choose an animal from a list of options and answer the essential question about how that animal adapts to its environment: *How do physical and behavioral traits help your animal to survive?* Finally, they select how they want to share their learning from a menu of options.

This choose-your-path format takes time to design, but it provides students all of the resources, media, structure, and choice they need to be successful. As students self-pace through the choose-your-path learning experience, you are freed to meet with individual students to get to know them, discuss their goals, and get a clear sense of their motivation. This time is invaluable to you as the facilitator of learning. It also communicates to every student that you care about them as individuals and want to help them to be successful in your class.

Teachers can use the goal-setting exercise described in Chapter 6 to anchor these early conversations with students.

- What do you want to achieve—academically, personally, or behaviorally?
- Why do you want to achieve these things?
- What is valuable about these goals from your perspective?

This provides insight into what our students care about as individuals. Then, as their coaches or facilitators, we can leverage their specific motivators to encourage them to lean in, take risks, and invest their time and energy resources into learning.

PRIORITIZE FEEDBACK TO SUPPORT STUDENTS AS THEY WORK. Feedback is one of the most powerful tools we have in our teaching tool belts for guiding learners toward mastery. Without feedback, students do not have a clear sense of what they are doing well, what they need to focus on, and what they can do to improve.

Despite the power of timely and actionable feedback, it is easy to neglect. Providing feedback is time-consuming and often takes a back seat to other aspects of our work. We must find a way to give feedback that is sustainable and effective. In the absence of face-to-face classes, teachers can communicate that they care about their students' progress by providing them with feedback on their work. When done well, feedback can strengthen the relationship that blended and online teachers have with their students.

Part of the reason feedback falls to the wayside is that it typically follows educators into their lives beyond school hours. Too often students complete work in isolation, teachers collect that work and provide feedback in isolation, and they return that work and expect students to process that feedback in isolation. This workflow does not create space for a *conversation* about the students' progress.

Balance with Blended Learning identifies many of the challenges associated with traditional approaches to feedback.[5] For example, feedback is often given on finished products when there is no incentive to act on the feedback to improve the work. If students are not required to take the feedback and do something with it, then the time we invest in providing that feedback isn't likely to move the needle in terms of the students' skills or abilities. Instead, find ways to pull feedback into the classroom to provide consistent, timely, focused, and actionable feedback *as* students work.

Save Time, Find Balance

Catlin

Several years ago, I made the decision to stop taking piles of student work home. I was tired of spending my evenings and weekends hunched over my computer giving students feedback on their work. Instead, I was going to use blended learning models to design lessons that allowed me to give real-time feedback *as* students worked. Instead of using my teacher-led station to explain how to write a thesis statement, structure a paragraph, or analyze a quote, I flipped my instruction and recorded videos. If all of my students needed to learn about the same five strategies for hooking their readers at the start of an introduction paragraph, I would record a video and let them control the pace of that experience. The less time I spent *talking*, the more time I had to work *with* students.

I began to dedicate my teacher-led station in our station rotation lessons to supporting my students as they wrote. This demanded that I embrace a new approach to giving feedback. I did not have time to give feedback on every aspect of their writing. Instead, I had to identify the specific aspect of their writing that I was going to give feedback on in a given station rotation lesson (e.g., thesis statements, topic sentences, or analysis). I did not attempt to fix every mechanical error in their writing (that was tough!). I had to stay focused. In a teacher-led station that spanned twenty-five minutes, I might have seven students who needed feedback.

At the start of the station, I explained the process and the focus of the real-time feedback session to my group. Students would continue working on their essays, and I would pop in and out of their digital documents, giving feedback on one aspect of their writing. If they had a question, I asked them to put it in a comment in their digital document instead of interrupting me. I knew I would never get through all of the students' papers if they were allowed to stop me and ask questions.

Over time, I got better at giving focused, actionable feedback as students wrote. I remember having students say to me, "This is the most feedback I've ever gotten on my writing!" Not only did I stop taking mountains of work home, my students appreciated being present for the process. They were able to immediately act on the comments and suggestions to improve their writing. Just as my coach ran beside me, suggesting subtle modifications to my form, teachers must sit beside students and provide focused feedback as they apply what they are learning. It is when students, or runners, attempt to put what they're learning into action that they are likely to trip, fall, and need support. That's why real-time feedback is so powerful. It shifts our focus from the product to the process.

Mastery-Oriented Feedback

In order to build student engagement in UDL, we need to provide numerous opportunities to provide mastery-oriented feedback. The teaching and learning landscape we are in will impact the type of feedback that works best to support students in making progress. Research indicates that using media, beyond text comments, positively impacts the students' perception of the quality of feedback they are receiving when they are working online. Online students who received audio or video feedback perceived that feedback as more thorough, detailed, and personal than text feedback. Students also reported being more motivated by audio and video feedback because they felt it was more clear and personalized. Interestingly, teachers also reported higher levels of engagement when giving video and audio feedback.[6]

Teachers working in blended learning environments, or entirely online, should consider scheduling real-time feedback sessions using videoconferencing software or recording video feedback or audio comments. These strategies are more likely to make feedback feel personal and motivate learners to act on the feedback they receive.

PRESENT CHALLENGING TASKS WITHIN EACH STUDENT'S ZONE OF PROXIMAL DEVELOPMENT. Imagine a learner at the center of the three concentric circles shown in figure 5.1. The inner circle closest to the learner symbolizes what they can do on their own without the support or guidance of a coach or teacher. The middle circle represents what that learner is capable of doing with support and guidance. The outer circle signifies what the learner is not yet capable of, even with support.

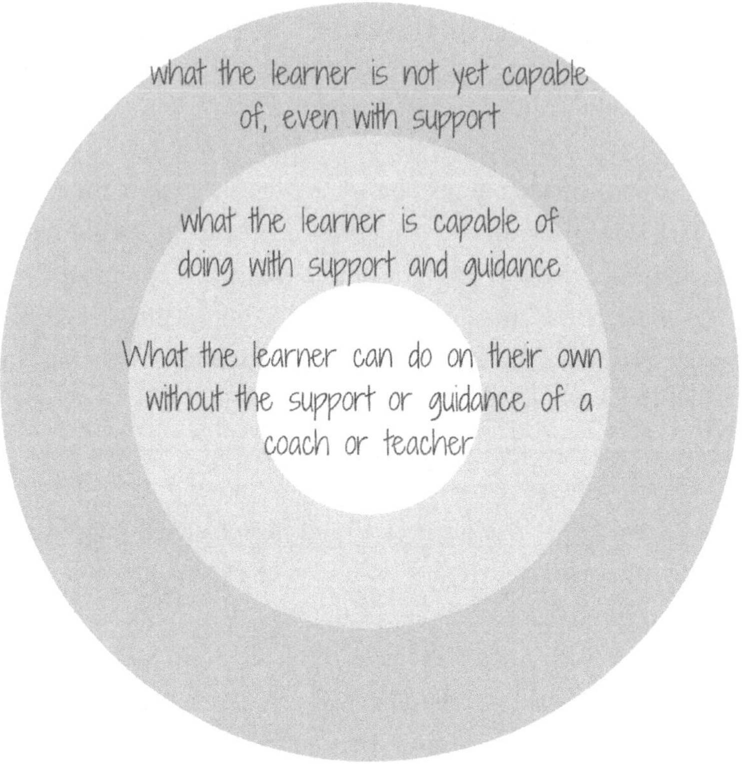

what the learner is not yet capable of, even with support

what the learner is capable of doing with support and guidance

What the learner can do on their own without the support or guidance of a coach or teacher

Figure 5.1: Zone of Proximal Development

It is our job to know our students' skills and abilities well enough to present them with challenging tasks that push them to continue growing and making progress. However, those tasks must be within their zones of proximal development, or they may get frustrated, feel discouraged, or give up.[7] This requires that we consistently monitor and track our students' progress to understand where each learner is in their journey toward understanding key concepts and mastering specific skills. Collecting formative assessment data, giving feedback as students work, and conferencing with students all help us to understand the variability of our classroom and how we can support specific learners.

They may not know how capable they are, so it's our job to let them know that we believe in them and we are there to support them.

Just like Benny the pigeon, our students can accomplish incredible feats if their facilitators believe in them, support them, and gradually teach them how to take responsibility for reaching their goal.

Cultivating a Community of Inquiry in Your Classroom

We are called to facilitate meaningful learning experiences for students. This requires that we connect with our learners, but it is equally as important that students feel connected to each other. The community of inquiry (CoI) theoretical framework was developed to understand the unique nature of teaching and learning in online and blended learning environments and, as a result, grounds much of the research on online and blended learning. The CoI provides educators with a structure to think about building an online learning community where students can collaborate and learn.

The CoI is composed of three overlapping presences: the social presence, the teaching presence, and the cognitive presence, as pictured in figure 5.2.[8] These three presences work in concert to cultivate a learning community that support students in pursuing inquiry and constructing knowledge.[9]

A key aspect of a high-functioning learning community is a strong social presence. The social presence is the students' ability to project their social and emotional selves in blended or online classes.[10] To successfully construct knowledge as part of a dynamic learning community, students need to view their classmates as real people with beliefs, values, and feelings, even if they are learning, in part or entirely, online. The physical distance between students in a blended learning or online course and the fact that more of their interactions are mediated by a screen can make developing a social presence challenging. However, the time spent developing a social presence has been shown to positively impact student engagement

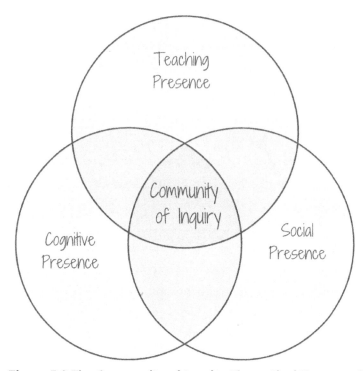

Figure 5.2 The Community of Inquiry Theoretical Framework

and participation, learner satisfaction with a course, and the quality of perceived learning.[11] Given the positive effects of a strong social presence on both engagement and learning, teachers have a powerful incentive to cultivate this dimension of their learning community.

The social presence is composed of three behaviors, which include:

- the expression of values, beliefs, and feelings
- open and purposeful communication among learners
- a sense of group cohesion, or feeling of connectedness to the learning community[12]

Let's explore concrete ways you can use your facilitation skills to promote these three behaviors to develop a strong social presence regardless of the learning landscape.

EXPRESSING VALUES, BELIEFS, AND FEELINGS. The expression of values, beliefs, and feelings requires a degree of vulnerability, so students need to feel safe expressing themselves. So, it's important to begin by establishing class agreements and norms.

- What do the members of the learning community agree to do? What actions and behaviors will keep the learning environment—on- and offline—feeling safe, supportive, respectful, and productive?
- What do the members of the learning community agree to avoid doing? What actions or behaviors might jeopardize the safety and productivity of the learning environment?
- What are appropriate consequences for students who violate the norms or jeopardize the safe space in class or online? How will the community handle that?

Often the teacher creates a list of expectations at the start of a school year and gives them to students on a syllabus or reviews them the first day of class. However, that approach does not include the learners or capitalize on their past experiences participating in learning communities. They know what makes them feel safe expressing their ideas and feelings, so asking them to help construct the list of agreements is a simple way to engage their voices and give them ownership over this process. When students play an active role in articulating expectations for behavior and potential consequences for missteps, they are more likely to comply with the established expectations and agreements.

Once clear agreements have been established, then the learning community must spend time getting to know one another. Icebreakers, check-in routines, and informal chats can all help students to build relationships and begin to see their peers as real people, even if they are interacting online. Teachers can take classic icebreakers, like two truths and a lie, and adapt them for the online environment. They can ask students to record videos sharing their three statements and guess each other's lies.

Teachers can group students in class or in breakout rooms to discuss questions like:

- If you could have lunch with a famous person—dead or alive—who would you choose and what three questions would you ask them?
- If you could travel in time, when and where would you go? What would you like to do there? Who would you like to meet?
- If you had to spend three months alone on a desert island, what three items would you bring and why?

In an entirely online class, these conversations can take place asynchronously in a text-based or video-based discussion. The goal of these fun, informal conversations is to get students comfortable engaging with each other, so that when the discussions become more academic in nature the students feel safe taking risks and sharing their ideas and opinions.

A simple check-in routine at the start of each class can also help students connect on an emotional level. Brené Brown is a research professor at the University of Houston and an expert on courage, shame, vulnerability, and empathy. Brown uses a two-word feeling check-in to begin her team's online meetings. Brown knows that when you ask someone, "How are you feeling?" you'll usually get a knee-jerk response like "I'm okay." To get a more accurate read on how her team members are feeling in a given moment, she asks them to share two words that encapsulate how they are feeling. They can be two totally different words, like stressed and hopeful. The goal is to create space for however people are feeling, and the beauty of this strategy is twofold: "First, it's super short. It doesn't take long for everyone to give their answer. It gives permission for people to quickly name their feelings without judgment. Second, it acknowledges that we humans often feel many things at once."[13]

You can also use a high-low structure to facilitate a check-in with students at the beginning or end of a class to get a sense of what is going well (the high) and what they are struggling with (the low). The high is something students are doing well, feeling confident about, or enjoying. The low is something they are struggling with, frustrated by, or confused about. Not only does this help students see that they are not alone in their struggles and that everyone has lows, it also provides the teacher with powerful formative assessment data. If multiple students are struggling with a concept, skill, or assignment, that is an indication that the teacher may need to pull those students into a small-group session to offer additional support.

OPEN AND PURPOSEFUL COMMUNICATION AMONG LEARNERS.
Discussion is a cornerstone of any academic course, regardless of the age of the learner or the subject area. Discourse helps learners construct and confirm meaning. Discussions expose students to different perspectives, encourage inquiry, and challenge them to make connections, orienting new learning in relation to existing knowledge. Discussion can be used to drive higher-order thinking and improve both understanding and retention. Maybe most powerful is the fact that academic discourse shifts students from consumers of other people's ideas to producers of their own ideas. Given the importance of conversations, we need to design and facilitate these conversations.

Discussion can take many forms. You can use pair shares, small-group, or whole-class discussion. We prefer smaller groupings for real-time discussion, as they allow every student to have the opportunity to share their ideas. Whole-class real-time conversations often fail to engage every voice because of time constraints. It is also scary for shy or anxious students to jump into a whole-group discussion with thirty of their peers, as opposed to participating in a small-group discussion with six to eight classmates.

Four-corner conversations are great for encouraging small-group discussion among students. To do this, you can randomly count students off by fours, intentionally mixing up the groups each time. The ones would go to one corner, the twos to another corner, and so on. They arrange their chairs in a circle and have ten to fifteen minutes to discuss a topic, text, or issue. You can listen and observe students in these conversations and provide feedback when necessary. This routine can support students in developing a deeper understanding of the course content, forming relationships with their classmates, and feeling more comfortable taking risks and sharing their ideas.

Online discussions are a staple of any blended learning or online course. Online discussions can happen synchronously during a videoconferencing session in breakout rooms or asynchronously in the form of text-based or video-based discussions. You can utilize the discussion functionality of your learning management system for older students with strong keyboarding skills. If you are working with younger learners, or learners who do not have strong keyboarding skills, you may have more success with video-based discussions. Online discussions build community, but they also challenge learners to develop their writing skills in a text-based discussion and their speaking and listening skills in a video-based discussion. These skills will take time to develop, and students will benefit from explicit instruction on how to successfully navigate online conversations.

A SENSE OF GROUP COHESION. It's important that students feel connected to a learning community. Teachers can facilitate group cohesion through interactions and engagement among the members of the class. The pandemic presented new barriers to student engagement, as classes shifted online and the lack of physical proximity made collaboration more challenging to facilitate. Luckily, technology provides multiple avenues to engage students in social learning spaces online.

Virtual social learning spaces create opportunities for the social and academic aspects of learning to collide. Social learning spaces "provide a place for students to interact with their peers . . . and take command over their own learning."[14] These spaces provide an avenue for students to learn with and from each other. The trick is identifying a virtual learning space that will work for your students given their age and the technology tools available to them.

Once teachers have identified the virtual spaces where students can connect synchronously (e.g., breakout rooms) or asynchronously (e.g., virtual Post-it note walls, shared digital documents or slide decks), they must create opportunities for students to work together. Collaboration, conversation, group work, jigsaw activities, carousel brainstorms, and project-based learning are strategies teachers can use to help students feel connected to the other members of the learning community. The more learners have to lean on one another and use each other as resources, the more likely they are to feel a strong sense of group cohesion.

Developing a dynamic learning community and cultivating a strong social presence in a class won't happen overnight. It requires a strong facilitator who can guide the group's interactions to ensure that agreements are upheld, students feel safe taking risks and sharing their ideas, and groups of learners can navigate shared tasks in a respectful and productive way.

SUMMARIZE, REFLECT, AND DISCUSS

Allowing students to self-direct their learning doesn't mean that we will have students "flying off" on their own like Benny the pigeon. We play a critical role as coaches and facilitators of learning. We have to commit to promoting participation, ensuring equity, and building trust. Not only do we have to continue to nurture relationships with students, but we have to shift the culture of the learning environment so students are willing to share authentic feedback, take risks, and take more ownership of their learning. Equally important, we need to create a space where students can reflect on focused, actionable feedback as they become more expert in their learning.

- How is being an effective facilitator of learning like being an effective coach?
- Effective facilitation requires educators to promote participation, ensure equity, and build trust. What are some strategies that you could implement in your practice to grow as a facilitator of learning?
- Being a facilitator of learning requires us to provide focused, actionable feedback to our learners. How do you currently provide feedback to your learners? And how do you ensure that learners are using the feedback to become more expert learners?

CHAPTER 6

Metacognitive Skill Building

Expert Learning and the *New York Times* Crossword Puzzle

Katie

The *New York Times* (*NYT*) wasn't always a fan of crossword puzzles. As the story goes, crossword puzzles were all the rage in the early 1900s, but the *Times* thought so little of the puzzles that they refused to publish them. Their tune changed, however, after the bombing of Pearl Harbor.

In a memo sent to his publisher, Lester Markel, the Sunday editor, noted, "We ought to proceed with the puzzle, especially in view of the fact it is possible there will now be bleak blackout hours—or if not that then certainly a need for relaxation of some kind or other."[1] And from there, the *New York Times* crossword puzzle was born.

Growing up, I had a fascination with the *NYT* puzzles, thanks to my grandmother. Every Sunday, we drove an hour to visit Gram.

When we got there, she would be parked on the couch, her nyloned feet curled beneath her, the Patriots pregame blaring too loudly from the TV. There she sat, her parakeet, Patrick, on her shoulder, a dictionary nearby, her pencil tapping on the tray table as she lost herself in the *NYT* Sunday puzzle.

Because it's in our blood, or because we are little old ladies in forty-somethings' bodies, my sister and I complete the *New York Times* crossword puzzle every day. As soon as I wake up every morning, I open up the *NYT* app, and start the puzzle. We both try on our own for a while, and when the kids start school, we connect to share clues if we haven't solved it. Every week, we get better and faster. Maybe someday, we will be able to solve the Saturday puzzle.

For puzzle enthusiasts, completing the *NYT* Saturday puzzle, without help, is bucket-list worthy. The puzzles get increasingly difficult throughout the week. On Monday, we can usually both finish in fifteen minutes—no help. On Saturday, we are on the phone for an hour or more and ultimately have to Google many of the clues.

Here's the thing about crossword puzzles—if you want to get good at them, you have to be willing to be wrong, or get stuck, a lot. You have to be committed to learning new words, asking questions, and solving problems. It involves an incredible amount of attention, thinking, and reflection. There is the fabulous frustration of trying to solve a puzzle and the moment of joy when you get it right. Learning is a lot like that. In many ways, meeting the needs of students requires us to try new things, reflect, and change our approaches.

How often do we, in our own practice, reflect and realize we have to do an about-face? I know that many times in my career, I have made changes, abandoned practices, and recognized that my previously held beliefs were simply false. The *NYT* was wrong about crossword puzzles, and they had to make a change. But thank goodness (for me!), they reflected and were willing to make that change. In order to serve the learners in front of us, we have to pivot, problem-solve, and confront previously held beliefs about teaching and learning.

The Value of Metacognition

The fundamental shift in control from teacher to learner at the heart of universally designed blended learning requires that students develop the skills necessary to share the responsibility for their learning. To do so, students must develop their self-regulation skills and hone their metacognitive muscles. This ability to regulate one's behavior and think about their thinking aids academic success and is particularly important for students learning at least in part online.[2] The increased autonomy inherent to blended and online learning requires that students have the skills necessary to make key decisions and advocate for themselves as learners. They must be comfortable thinking about their learning and developing a deeper understanding of themselves as students.

The benefits of metacognitive skill building are not reserved for older kids. In a study of metacognition in early childhood education, researchers found that children as young as three years old were "capable of developing fundamental forms of metacognition."[3] The investment in helping students develop these metacognitive skills pays off in spades because students who are comfortable using their metacognitive skills are more "strategic, flexible, and productive in their learning process."[4] Teachers want to cultivate independent students capable of tackling unfamiliar problems and tasks; however, to do so requires the ability to think about their thinking and learning with intentionality.

Building metacognition is necessary for effective expert learning. This skill is critical to engaging our students in meaningful, self-directed learning before, during, and after universally designed lessons. It includes three specific cognitive strategies: meta-attention, metacomprehension, and metacognitive reflection.[5]

- Before a lesson: Meta-attention: What are my goals?
- During a lesson: Metacomprehension: Where am I now?
- After a lesson: Metacognitive reflection: What would I do differently next time?

By incorporating the strategies outlined in this chapter, you will have a strategy to ensure that students are building these three strategies, which will support them in becoming purposeful, resourceful, and strategic learners. But remember, this work takes practice. Just like any muscle in the body, our metacognitive muscles require exercise.

Building My Rowing Muscles

Catlin

When the pandemic began in 2020 and my gym closed, I splurged on a rower for my garage. I had used the rower at my gym a handful of times, but I was not in rowing shape when it arrived. The first few weeks were tough. I could barely row for ten minutes. My breathing was ragged, and my arms and back felt like they were on fire. I stuck with it despite the initial physical discomfort because, quite frankly, I didn't have another option. After two weeks of rowing every other day, I hit three thousand meters rowing for fifteen minutes straight!

As the weeks turned into months and the pandemic dragged on, my rowing became less labored. I rowed with more ease and confidence. My body adapted to the demands of the rower, developing the muscles I needed to thrive on the machine. The same development can happen in our students when we provide the tools, routines, and guidance to help them begin thinking about their learning.

Fostering Metacognition the UDL/Blended Learning Way

Teachers can help students to become expert learners and develop the skills necessary to plan, monitor, and reflect on their learning with regular routines, modeling, and practice. We want you to think about metacognitive skill-building in three distinct parts: before, during, and after each lesson. These stages correspond to the three strategies inherent in metacognition: meta-attention, metacomprehension, and metacognitive reflection.

Before: Meta-Attention

Meta-attention is a student's awareness of the learning goal, which helps them focus and manage their attention to the learning activity. UDL is about "firm goals and flexible means," and making these goals clear to students can support their meta-attention. Additionally, flexibility means requiring students to self-differentiate their learning to work toward the goal, so consistent reminders about learning outcomes allow students to make better, more effective decisions about their learning. Oftentimes, when educators learn about UDL and blended learning, they consider offering options and choices for students. One common concern is that students will not make appropriate decisions for their learning. This, however, is alterable when we take the time to share the goal of learning and why it's important *and* when we provide students time to create a plan for achieving it and consistently monitor their progress.

In traditional classrooms, students receive learning objectives, instructions, and assignments. They are told what to do and how to do it. However, to be our partners in learning as UDL and blended learning demands, they must develop their self-regulation and metacognitive skills. Students need opportunities to think about what *they* want to achieve, how they want to work toward goals *they* care about, and how *they* want to approach particular assignments.

SETTING GOALS. The first step in helping students to think about their learning is to teach them how to set academic, personal, and behavioral goals. What do they care about? What would they like to accomplish? What would be meaningful for them to work toward?

When working with students, you can simplify the goal-setting process by breaking it down into three parts.

- Where are you going? What are you working toward?
- How will you get there? What actions or behaviors will help you to make progress toward these goals?
- How will you know when you've arrived? What will success look or feel like?

WHERE ARE YOU GOING? This question prompts students to identify the specific goals they value and want to work toward. Allowing students to decide what combination of academic, personal, and behavior goals they want to articulate may result in more buy-in from them. Adding personal goals may help them feel more invested in this exercise and develop a goal-setting strategy they carry into their lives beyond school.

HOW WILL YOU GET THERE? This is the most challenging step in the goal-setting process for most students. They have to articulate specific steps, behaviors, or actions they believe will help them to make progress toward their goals. These behaviors and actions are what will require students to develop their self-regulation skills to ensure that their conduct and choices are aligned with their goals. This may require personal sacrifices, like spending less time watching television, playing video games, or chatting with friends online.

HOW WILL YOU KNOW WHEN YOU'VE ARRIVED? The final step in the goal-setting process challenges students to imagine reaching the goal, or goals, they have set for themselves and articulate what that will look or feel like. Will there be an external marker that they have been successful, like a grade or more playing time? Will there be an internal indication that they expect to experience when they reach this goal, like a feeling of pride or satisfaction? It is important for students to imagine this moment and how they'll feel, as it will serve to motivate them to do the hard work of reaching their goals.

Setting goals gives students a voice in articulating learning objectives that extend beyond the curriculum. It creates space for what they care about. It's a simple and sustainable way to prioritize their agency in the learning process. Goals can positively impact motivation by helping students to consider how their behaviors align (or not) with their goals.[6] If students see how the work they do in classrooms impacts their ability to make progress toward their goals, they are more likely to feel invested in that work.

PLANNING AND STRATEGIZING. Students also need opportunities to think about how they want to approach a particular task *before* they get started. This helps learners focus their attention. These opportunities to plan and think through strategy can help them to develop confidence in their abilities to navigate unfamiliar tasks or challenges. If students are not periodically challenged to think about how they want to approach a complex task, they may flounder when facing a new or novel situation.

Teachers can help cultivate more confident, resourceful, and strategic students by challenging them to think through the parts of a process in advance of starting to work. Students benefit from thinking through the steps they want to take, the strategies they want to use, and the resources they have at their disposal in advance. Here are questions students can ask themselves while planning their tasks:

- What steps will you take to complete this assignment or project?
- What strategies can you use to approach this particular task? What have you done in the past that might work in this situation?
- What aspects of the assignment or project may present challenges? Do you think you will need help or support as you work through a particular aspect of this task?
- If you get stuck, what will you do? What resources do you have access to that might be helpful?

Teachers can ask individuals or groups of students to work through an assignment or project proposal to encourage them to think through these questions or invite them to write and post a learning blog at the start of their work, answering these questions. Not only do the answers to these questions help students to engage in metacognitive thinking at the start of the work, but it provides the teachers with invaluable information about where students are beginning in their work and where they may need additional instruction or support.

During: Metacomprehension

Metacomprehension is a process of assessing your level of understanding. When we provide options and pathways for students to learn, we hope they recognize when they are learning, and when they are struggling, so they can adjust midcourse. It would be awesome if learners were able to reflect and have a thought bubble that says, "Hmm, I am really struggling with this concept. I should try to learn this in another way or use one of the scaffolds available." But alas, that isn't often how it goes. Research suggests that most learners aren't super accurate when practicing metacomprehension. To support metacomprehension, it is critical that we design opportunities for students to reflect on and self-assess their learning throughout the learning process.

Too often, students move through a learning cycle or unit without appreciating either the benefit or impact of the work they are doing. Many of us have heard students groan about busywork. When students label a task as busywork, it is a sign that they do not understand the purpose of that work. Despite our best intentions, we sometimes fail to make the value of the work we design clear to learners.

This is a common phenomenon in education. Teachers understand why they are doing what they are doing and what objectives the class is working toward, yet the why behind the work may not be clear to students. One way to combat this disconnect is to teach students how to monitor and track their progress.

ONGOING SELF-ASSESSMENT. An ongoing self-assessment routine requires that students spend time each week thinking about their work and monitoring their progress toward specific standards or skills. In order to understand their progress, they select a piece of work from the week, align it to a specific standard or skill, evaluate their level of mastery on a scale from 1 to 4, and write a brief explanation of why they gave themselves a specific assessment score.

At the start of each learning cycle or unit, the teacher identifies target standards and skills. This creates clarity about what the teacher and the students are working on in a given cycle or unit. It is important that the language of the target standards and skills is "student-friendly." This may require that the teacher spend time rewording the standards using language students will understand.

Alternatively, teachers can challenge students to work in collaborative groups to rewrite the target standards in language that make sense to them.

The goal of an ongoing self-assessment exercise is to have students think critically about a specific piece of work they've produced to understand what it reveals about their development. Students are prompted to think about the following questions as they assess their work.

- Where would you put yourself on a scale from (1) beginning to (4) mastery?
- Why did you put yourself at this level of mastery?
- What do you see in your work that you believe demonstrates this level of mastery?
- What questions do you have about your work? What additional support might you need to continue improving this specific skill?

Use a simple four-point mastery scale, as pictured in figure 6.1, for self-assessment activities.

FOUR-POINT MASTERY SCALE		
1	Beginning	I cannot do this on my own. I need support from my teacher.
2	Developing	I'm getting the hang of it, but I may still need some support from my teacher and my classmates.
3	Proficient	I feel confident I can do this on my own without support.
4	Mastery	I feel extremely confident in my skills and abilities. I believe I am ready for another challenge.

Figure 6.1: Four-Point Mastery Scale

Teachers working with younger students may want to create a mastery scale that is visual, using emoji faces or hand signals to help students communicate how they are feeling about a particular assignment or skill, as shown in figure 6.2.

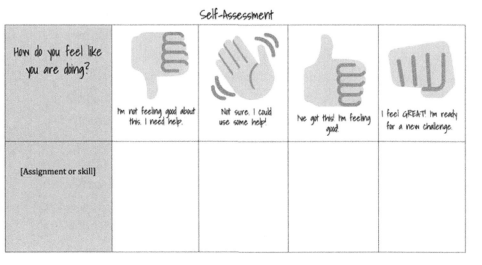

Figure 6.2: Visual Self-Assessment Scale

Regular self-assessment routines help students to develop cognitive awareness and build metacomprehension. They can more readily identify the areas where they feel strong versus the areas where they are struggling and need more practice or support. They begin to understand the value of the work they are doing and how specific assignments are helping them to improve their comprehension of key concepts or develop specific skills. Once students begin to appreciate the value of the work they are doing, they are less likely to label tasks as busywork and are more likely to invest time and energy into their assignments.

After: Metacognitive Reflection

Metacognitive reflection is when learners reflect on the process of learning so that they can transfer the skills for future use. When designing instruction, it is critical that we carve out time for students to reflect on the process of learning after a lesson. During metacognitive reflection, we encourage students to reflect upon their learning by asking questions like "What worked?" "What didn't?" and "What would you do differently the next time?"

A reflective practice that takes place at the end of the learning cycle, unit, or large-scale assignment can positively impact academic achievement, cognitive awareness, and motivation.[7] This reflection can take many forms, but the goal is to carve out time to encourage students to reflect on their learning. Just as we are trained to end each unit with an assessment designed to measure what students know or can do, a reflective practice should be a consistent part of every learning cycle. Students must stop to reflect on what they learned, how they learned it, and what is still unclear.

REFLECTION. A reflective practice can take many forms, from a traditional journal to a podcast recording. Instead of requiring that all students reflect in the same way, this is an opportunity to universally design the reflection and utilize a range of online and offline tools to allow students to select from a range of strategies (see figure 6.3). Some students may prefer to reflect in writing while others may enjoy a more artistic approach, using drawings or sketches to reflect on what they learned and how this new learning connects to their prior knowledge.

Figure 6.3: Multiple Means of Reflection

GROWTH OVER TIME. A growth-over-time exercise asks students to compare work they've produced from two different moments in a grading period, semester, or school year. Students rarely revisit previous work, yet it is in a close examination of work done at different moments in time when their growth and development are most striking.

A simple growth-over-time activity, like the one pictured in figure 6.4, is one way to encourage a reflective practice aimed at helping students to identify specific areas of growth and improvement. Students select a piece of work from the beginning of the grading period, semester, or school year and consider the following questions:

- What skills are evident in this work?
- What did you do well in this piece?
- What errors do you see in your work?
- Is there anything surprising about the quality of your work?

After the student has spent time with this initial piece, they repeat the process with a second work sample that they produced more recently. Ideally, this is a piece of work that the student feels reflects their skills and abilities right now. They examine the second piece, answering the same questions.

The third and final step asks them to compare these two pieces of work to identify specific areas of improvement and growth. They are prompted to answer the following questions:

- What do you notice about the changes in your work?
- How have your skills changed and developed?
- Where is your growth as a learner most evident? What do you think contributed to your growth? What helped you improve over time?
- What does comparing these two pieces of work reveal about you as a learner?

GROWTH OVER TIME	
Select one piece of work from the beginning of the semester to analyze. • What skills are evident in this work? • What did you do well? • What errors do you see in your work? • Is there anything surprising about the quality of your work?	Select one piece of work from the end of the semester to analyze. • What skills are evident in this work? • What did you do well? • What errors do you see in your work? • Is there anything surprising about the quality of your work?
Compare these two pieces of work—one from the beginning of the semester and one from this week. • What do you notice about the changes in your work? • How have your skills changed and developed? • Where is your growth as a learner most evident? What do you think contributed most to your growth this year? • What does comparing these two pieces of work reveal about you as a learner?	

Figure 6.4: Growth-over-Time Activity

As students work through this growth-over-time activity, you will hear exclamations: "Oh my gosh! I cannot believe I wrote this!" "This is embarrassing. There are so many mistakes in this one!" "Wow, I can't believe how much better this is!" Remind your students that learning is a process, so it is normal for work done early in the process to have mistakes. Encourage them to focus on their growth and appreciate the impact that their hard work has had on their development. It's rewarding to see kids stand a little taller after this exercise because they feel a sense of pride and accomplishment.

All of these routines take time and practice. In the day-to-day scramble to cover curriculum, routines like the ones described in this chapter are easy to neglect. However, teachers using universally designed blended learning models can lean on these models to create space for metacognitive skill-building.

SUMMARIZE, REFLECT, AND DISCUSS

As educators, we have the power and privilege to design learning experiences that help students learn how to learn. The three UDL principles were designed to ensure that all students become expert learners. This is completely transformative because, in the past, the main goal of school was teaching content. Through UDL and blended learning, we shift our focus from teaching content to teaching learning.

As we shared at the beginning of the chapter, the *New York Times* did not set out to publish crossword puzzles, but they reflected and recognized that they needed to adapt. We must find inspiration in Lester Markel's memo, where he recognized that the paper needed to shift its previous practice and stance and try something new. The same is true in our classrooms.

The shift in control from teacher to learner that drives both Universal Design for Learning and blended learning requires that students develop the skills necessary to share the responsibility for their learning. When we model metacognition and design opportunities for students to set goals, monitor their progress, and reflect on their learning, we are creating opportunities for students to learn who they are as learners so they can transfer their skills to the goals that are most important to them. Hey, maybe someday they will set out to solve the Saturday crossword puzzle. And if they do, they will have the tools they need to cross that bad boy off their bucket list.

- To help students develop as expert learners, we have to support them in metacognitive skill-building, which is the ongoing process of asking three questions: *What are my goals? Where am I now? What would I do differently the next time?* Which of these questions do your learners struggle with the most? Which do you struggle with the most?
- Metacognitive skill-building is embedded before, during, and after each instructional activity. Consider where and how you currently support student metacognition and then note any ahas or affirmations from this chapter.
- What strategies outlined in this chapter will you implement to support students in becoming purposeful, resourceful, and strategic learners?

CHAPTER 7

Assessments for and with Learners

Sad Santiago Puppets

Katie

As a seventh-grade teacher, I taught *The Old Man and the Sea*. Before I learned about Universal Design for Learning (UDL), I taught the book exactly as it had been taught for decades before me: assign reading, give multiple-choice quiz on reading, discuss text, repeat. At the end, I dusted off the multiple-choice test from the filing cabinet, added a prompt for a five-paragraph essay, and let kids go to town.

To be honest, I didn't look at the standards, or articulate any clear goals, before designing the test. But during the summer of 2009, I attended a weeklong professional development institute on Universal Design for Learning (UDL), and I began to see just how many barriers were present in my assessment design. I wanted to do better, but in hindsight, I didn't quite know how.

I started on the right track by focusing on "firm goals," but I didn't quite make it to flexible means. My first foray into UDL resulted in selecting a standard that would drive instruction for *The Old Man and the Sea*. I opened up the state framework, and much like I was playing Pin the Tail on the Donkey, I picked one: Analyze how particular elements of a story or drama interact (e.g., how setting shapes the characters or plot). The instruction I provided was much more on target. We closely read short, profound excerpts of the text and focused on how the days out at sea changed the protagonist, Santiago. I encouraged students to think about the setting around them and how it impacted them and changed them. As much as I started with backward design, I never quite made it to providing a universally designed assessment.

The revision of the multiple-choice megatest was the Santiago puppet project, which took way too much class time and created additional barriers for student learning. In this project, I asked all students to trace a paper doll cutout of Santiago on a poster board. On his head, they wrote quotes about what he thought; on his chest, they wrote quotes about how he felt; and on his hands, they wrote quotes about what he did. Boom—characterization focus! Then, we spent days cutting and gluing, creating frayed clothes out of old denim and meticulously tracing the quotes in black Sharpie markers.

Standards-based? Slightly. Fun? Maybe. Universally designed? No. I had taken a one-size-fits-all assessment and turned it into another (albeit more artistic) one-size-fits-all assessment. And the assessment lacked construct validity. A valid assessment adequately covers the targeted learning outcomes and provides students with opportunities to show their knowledge of concepts in many different ways and with multiple measures, to establish a composite picture of student learning.

My sad Santiago puppets did nothing of the sort. All I knew is that my students could cut and trace quotes with Sharpie. And while

I'm kicking myself in hindsight, I recognize that I put so much effort into the summative assessment that I missed incredible opportunities to support student reflection, self-assessment, and expert learning while they were learning about characterization. In short, I was so focused on designing assessments *of* learning that I often failed to design them *as*, or *for*, learning.

The Power of Formative Assessment

"Effective assessment practices support better communication about learning between students and teachers."[1] We love this sentiment, yet we don't think it is how most students view assessment. Too often, traditional approaches to assessment result in resentment and can actually damage the student-teacher relationship. Traditional approaches to assessing students' work lack transparency. It's not uncommon for teachers to spend countless hours of their evenings and weekends grading student work. The data collected as a result of grading student work is often unclear or even unknown to students.

We often talk about assessments as being diagnostic, formative, and summative. Lorna Earl and Steven Katz, faculty members at the University of Toronto and leaders in the field of data-driven instruction, make a distinction between types of assessments by articulating their purposes more clearly. They categorize assessments as being *assessment of*, *assessment for*, and *assessment as* learning.[2] *Assessment of* learning is summative—for grading and reporting like my mega-multiple-choice test and the two-week paper doll project. *Assessment for* and *assessment as* learning, however, recognize the power of ongoing diagnostic and formative assessment to drive student autonomy, reflection, and learning in authentic, valid, and innovative ways.

Assessment for learning is designed to give learners and teachers information to modify and differentiate teaching and learning activities, to streamline and target instruction and resources, and to provide mastery-oriented feedback to students to help them advance their learning.

Assessment as learning is a process of developing and supporting metacognition for students. When students are active, engaged, and critical assessors, whether through self-assessment, self-reflection, or self-reported grading, they can build comprehension, relate it to prior knowledge, and use it to make decisions about their learning.

Although the UDL framework recognizes there is a place for summative assessments, the model favors formative assessments that are planned and intentionally part of ongoing instruction. The founders of UDL are clear: "We believe well-crafted, thoughtful summative assessments can be important but only when used in conjunction with an array of other types of assessments designed to improve both teaching and learning."[3]

We work with teachers around the world who recognize their assessments need to better meet the needs of learners. But there is often a question of how. First things first—UDL and blended learning are not fun meters. They are not about replacing one inaccessible assessment with another. Instead, it's about unpacking standards, removing irrelevant constructs to increase the validity of the assessment, and backward designing multiple assessments where students have flexibility to express what they know throughout the learning experience, not just at the end.

Designing assessments using the principles of UDL requires a focus on providing alternate pathways to engage students, pathways to help them to build comprehension and understanding, and pathways that allow them to express how they have met the standard in flexible ways.

When creating learning experiences through the UDL lens, educators should start with the standard and work backward. It's wise to begin by determining the type of standard a student is expected to meet before creating multiple pathways for students to self-assess and monitor their progress.

There are two types of standards, and the distinction is critical for determining which options and choices are appropriate and valid. If the standard is a content standard, the student will need to demonstrate that he or she knows something or has attained knowledge. For example, your student may need to know what photosynthesis is and how it works, identify factors leading to the start of the Civil War, or be able to explain characterization or the Fibonacci sequence.

If the standard is a method standard, on the other hand, the learner will need to demonstrate that he or she has learned to do something and has attained a skill. Method standards are action oriented: learners may need to know how to divide with decimal points, write an argument, conduct a series of steps for a scientific experiment, or play an instrument.

When creating universally designed learning assessments, educators should ask themselves: "At the end of this lesson, unit, or professional development series, what do my learners have to know or what do they need to be able to do?" If you brainstorm all of the possible ways that a learner could potentially show you that they have met the standard and comprehend the information, you'll realize that there are more possibilities than you may have first imagined.

For example, if a learner needs to demonstrate that he has met a content standard, you could provide options for learners to present to peers, design an infographic, produce a short video, or write an essay or blog. There are so many options available for a learner to convey knowledge. In *The Old Man and the Sea* faux pas, students were analyzing the impact of plot and setting on character development. They didn't all have to create a giant Santiago puppet! Instead, they could have created a social media profile capturing the changes in Santiago over time with images and updates. They could have written a series of journal entries from Santiago's point of view at different points in the plot, providing the reader insight into his mental, emotional, and physical state. More artistically inclined students could have created a comic or graphic story, visually showing his evolution as a character. Students who enjoy performance could have acted out pivotal scenes from the text in character with moments where they break the fourth wall to provide the viewer with more insight into Santiago's character. The options for how students could have demonstrated their understanding of how the setting and plot impacted Santiago were limitless.

If you need a learner to demonstrate that she has met a method standard, you may not have the same level of flexibility with outcomes, but you have numerous opportunities to provide students with the option to work alone, work in a group, or to use exemplars, graphic organizers, assistive technology, or a math reference sheet. Essentially, you can ask yourself two questions when designing an assessment experience that will help you to determine "acceptable evidence" that is universally designed.

- What do learners need to know or be able to do?
- How will both the students and I know that they can do it?

The level of choices provided will be determined by the first question, or the standard. The important thing to remember is that while the standard or goal is firm, the means should always remain flexible when universally designing these experiences. But all choices are not equal.

There are many choice boards where there are numerous options and choices that are unrelated to the standard. Our best advice for this is to identify the learning goal at the top of the choice board or menu. As you reflect on each option, ask yourself, "Would this allow students and me to determine where they are in relation to the goal?" If the answer is no, send it to its grave with the Santiago puppet!

Assessment Is an Integral Part of Learning, Not an Add-On

Catlin

I attended a college preparatory high school in Southern California. It was an academically rigorous environment, laser-focused on preparing students for college, and the assessments attempted to mirror the terrifying experience of midterms and final exams that we would inevitably face at a university.

When I think back to my high school experience, the only methods my teachers used to evaluate what I knew or was able to do were essays, quizzes, and multiple-choice tests. I do not remember my teachers ever starting with a pre-assessment or diagnostic to understand where I was beginning. Since no pre-assessment data was collected, what we knew as individual learners did not drive the design of the learning experiences. Each class followed the exact one-size-fits-all approach from instruction through assessment. Assessment was not used *for* or *as* learning. It was entirely summative and, often, felt punitive.

I was a studious student in high school. I took assessments seriously, often staying up into the early morning hours studying concepts, vocabulary, processes, and formulas. I read our dense textbooks armed with highlighter, pen, and stacks of colorful Post-it notes. I created copious flashcards and spent days reviewing them. Yet I often felt like assessments were a game of gotcha. Teachers would ask questions that seemed designed to trip me up or ask about an obscure detail that didn't seem central to the unit of study. It was a frustrating and defeating experience as a student.

You'd think my negative experiences with assessment as a student would have inspired me to explore different approaches to evaluating my students' knowledge and skills when I became a teacher.

Unfortunately not. When I began my teaching career in 2002, I approached assessment in the same way I had experienced it as a student. I did not begin with a diagnostic or pre-assessment to better understand my students, because, quite frankly, the idea of using data to drive my design was not something I had been taught to do. In fact, in 2002, if someone had said to me, "Catlin, you should be attempting to personalize learning," I would have laughed. How on earth was I going to personalize learning for a class of thirty students? Let alone five classes of thirty students. It would have seemed like a herculean task. Yet I knew in those early years that the way I approached my work as a teacher was not meeting the needs of the vast majority of my students.

As I shifted from designing a single learning experience for the entire class to embracing blended learning, I realized I could differentiate for different groups of students with different needs and begin to imagine moving toward personalization, but assessment was the key to accomplishing those goals. Assessment is the driver of both differentiation (a teacher move) and personalization (a partnership between the teacher and learner) in a blended learning environment.

Without weaving assessment into every part of the learning process, teachers cannot design learning experiences to meet the wide range of needs in a class, make adjustments or modifications during the learning, or accurately measure progress toward stated learning objectives or goals. At all points in the design and facilitation process, teachers need to hungrily, strategically, and consistently collect data. As a result, assessment, in its various forms, must be present in each part of the teaching and learning process, as pictured in figure 7.1.

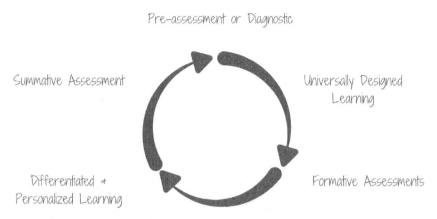

Pre-assessment or Diagnostic

Summative Assessment

Universally Designed Learning

Differentiated + Personalized Learning

Formative Assessments

Figure 7.1: The Role of Assessment in Teaching and Learning

Assessment for Learning

To cultivate an inclusive and equitable classroom that strives to meet the needs of individual learners and celebrates diversity, we must understand where our students are beginning their journeys. Learning isn't like a 100-meter sprint. Students do not line up shoulder to shoulder and begin from the same location. Some students will have an advantage that puts them out in front, while other students may be starting several paces behind the group.

When defining the attributes of an inclusive classroom, Spencer Salend, a professor at SUNY-New Paltz and author of *Creating Inclusive Classrooms: Effective and Reflective Practices*, says, "more than anything, it means taking into account the unique strengths and challenges of *all students* in today's diverse, inclusive classroom and using research-based, universally designed, and culturally responsive practices and assistive and instructional technologies that enhance learning."[4] The starting point for this work is a pre-assessment or diagnostic designed to provide data about the diversity of experiences and skills in our classrooms so we can use that data to inform our design (e.g., approach to instruction, grouping strategy, supports and scaffolds).

Since students don't all start with the same prior knowledge or skill sets, it is critical to begin with a pre-assessment or diagnostic as an assessment *for* learning to understand where they are starting from.

- What do students already know about a topic or subject?
- Where did this knowledge come from?
- What life experiences, skills, or world views are students bringing to the learning?
- What are their attitudes toward specific topics or subjects?

You can use a variety of strategies both online and offline to collect data to understand where students are beginning in terms of their prior knowledge and use that information to inform their design work. Below are some ways to assess what students know at the start of a learning cycle:

- **Connect the Dots:** Give students a collection of key terms or concepts and ask them to "connect the dots" with arrows, drawings, symbols, and explanations that show their relationship to one another. Be sure to universally design the experience and give your students options to connect the dots on paper or online using an infographic design tool.
- **Concept Map:** Ask students to surface what they know about a topic or subject in a visual concept map on paper or using a digital document.
- **Ninety-Second Brain Dump:** Give students ninety seconds to share everything they know about a topic, concept, vocabulary word, famous person, moment in history, type of writing, or scientific phenomenon in writing, on a digital document, or in a video recording.

- **Two-Minute Talks:** Pair students in class or online in breakout rooms and ask them to take turns (one minute per person) sharing everything they know about a topic. The teacher's job is to observe, listen, and learn. You can provide sentence stems as a scaffold!
- **Graphic Organizer or KWL:** Ask students to complete a graphic organizer or KWL chart capturing what they know about a topic and what they want to learn. This can be done verbally in class or digitally on a document or shared slide deck.

This pre-assessment data should also inform the ways in which teachers weave together active, engaged learning online and offline. Which blended learning model will be the best suited to meeting the diversity of needs in a classroom? If a concept or skill is new to the majority of the class, perhaps the whole-group rotation or a flipped classroom approach is more appropriate. However, if there is a dramatic difference in terms of prior knowledge and skill sets, the station rotation and playlist models may be a better fit since they provide the teacher with more opportunities to meet with and support small groups or individual learners.

Not only is using assessment critical to designing effective and differentiated learning experiences, it's impossible to know whether our design is effectively moving students toward learning objectives if we do not know where each student is starting the race.

Assessment as Learning

The beauty of formative assessments is that they are informal. They can be collected by simply listening to and observing students. It is incredible how much we can learn just by watching students work and using that data to make minor adjustments. As we navigate flexible learning landscapes, it is important to embrace formative assessment strategies that can work in person or online. Below is a collection of formative assessment strategies designed to check for understanding and identify gaps or misconceptions, so they can be addressed quickly.

It's important to note that teachers can use a combination of strategies to provide students with agency and choice. As we have highlighted throughout this book, not all students will thrive by expressing what they know in the same way. Some students will feel comfortable recording a video explanation, while others may prefer writing, drawing, or sketching a flowchart. So, if we want to gather accurate formative assessment data, we should avoid using a one-size-fits-all approach to formative assessment. Student agency over the method they use to share what they are learning, even informally during the learning, is likely to provide a more complete picture of where they are in their journey toward understanding key concepts and mastering specific skills. Teachers can present students with a menu of formative assessment options and allow them to select the one they feel is the best fit for them.

- **Quiz or polls:** Asking students to complete a short quiz or respond to a poll can provide quick data you can use to ensure students are comprehending key concepts while also surfacing areas of confusion. It's important to note, if you are using a quiz to collect formative assessment data, that you should *not* put that data or the score into a grade book.
- **3-2-1 activity:** The 3-2-1 structure is simple and versatile. Ask students to identify 3 things they learned, 2 connections they were able to make, and 1 question they still have. The prompts connected to each number can be altered depending on the lesson and what information would be most useful to the teacher. You may ask students to identify something that was surprising or provide examples of practical application. The 3-2-1 activity can be completed on paper,

or you can create a digital slide deck with enough slides so that each member of the class can capture their ideas on a slide. This way, students can see what other members of the class are saying and learn from one another online.

- **Tell me how or explain it to a friend.** This strategy is perfect for encouraging students to surface their thinking in recorded audio or videos. Instead of asking students to complete a set of problems or compose a writing sample, the teacher presents a problem or task and asks students to "tell me how" they would solve the problem or approach the task or "explain it to a friend." The goal is *not* to solve the problem or complete task, but rather to articulate the process they would use, step by step.

- **Quick writes:** Short-form written responses or summaries are another way to collect data about what students know or can do. You can present students with a prompt and give them a set amount of time (e.g., five or ten minutes) to respond on paper or a digital document. Encourage students to use accessibility tools like voice-to-text if writing creates a barrier.

- **What's this like? Create an analogy:** Just as we are using analogies throughout this book to make the ideas clear, relatable, and easier to remember (who is likely to forget the duck boat analogy?), you can challenge students to create an analogy to demonstrate their understanding of key concepts. A "what's this like?" check-in will help you gauge students' comprehension. Analogies can also help learners to retain what they are learning. The strongest analogies can be shared with the class to support deeper learning for everyone.

Just as chefs will dip a spoon into a sauce while it simmers to test the flavor, teachers need to build mechanisms into their lessons to collect informal data to understand student progress through a learning cycle. A chef may need to add additional ingredients or spices to the sauce to improve the flavor. Similarly, you may need to provide additional instruction, modeling, or scaffolds to support students in understanding key concepts or mastering specific skills, making their learning experience richer. The chef may need to turn up the heat to accelerate the cooking process or turn it down to give the sauce more time to simmer and the flavors more time to mingle. Similarly, formative assessment data may help you understand which students are ready to move on or tackle more challenging tasks, while identifying students who need a slower pace and more time to work with concepts or practice particular skills.

This information is critical if we are going to differentiate or personalize learning. If the formative assessment data collected indicates that a group of students is struggling with a specific concept or skill, you can provide small-group instruction or an optional skill station to clarify concepts, facilitate an interactive modeling session, guide additional practice, or provide the group with additional supports, like guided notes templates, sentence frames, a word bank with definitions, or additional examples.

Formative assessment data should be shared with students whenever possible. This informal data about their progress can be used to guide reflection or encourage students to think about what level of support they need to continue making progress toward their goals. When we make formative assessment data available to students, it becomes a tool *for* learning more about themselves—their progress, needs, strengths, and weaknesses.

Assessment of Learning

Summative assessments typically occur at the end of a learning cycle and provide the teacher, learner, and parents or guardians with information about student progress, growth, and levels of mastery. They are an assessment *of* learning. There are three types of summative assessments: traditional, alternative, and authentic.[5] Traditional assessments are the essays and multiple-choice exams that many of us grew up with and that we used early in our teaching careers before we embarked on our respective journeys into UDL and blended learning. Traditional forms of assessment may provide us with data that is useful, but these modes of assessment are unlikely to feel valuable or meaningful for students.

Alternative assessments offer diverse learners the opportunity to share what they know verbally through audio recordings or video, physically through a demonstration, or visually through drawings or artwork. Ideally, the student will enjoy flexible means or the agency to make choices about how *they* want to communicate what they know or share their learning.[6]

Authentic assessments present students with a task relevant to their lives. They may use alternative modes of expression, but the task at the heart of authentic assessments must be meaningful to the students to be truly authentic in nature.[7] These assessments often take the form of performance tasks or project-based learning (PBL).

Jay McTighe defines a performance task as "any learning activity or assessment that asks students to perform to demonstrate their knowledge, understanding and proficiency. Performance tasks yield a tangible product and/or performance that serve as evidence of learning. Unlike a selected-response item (e.g., multiple-choice or matching) that asks students to select from given alternatives, a performance task presents a situation that calls for learners to apply their learning in context."[8]

You can use performance tasks to give students more agency over their assessments, allowing them to make key decisions about how they want to perform or what they want to produce. The more agency students enjoy, the more likely they are to invest time and energy in a task. Since performance tasks require critical and creative thinking, flexibility, explanation, justification, and support, it is critical that students be invested in the process.

Project-based learning is "a teaching method in which students gain knowledge and skills by working for an extended period of time to investigate and respond to an authentic, engaging, and complex question, problem, or challenge."[9] Although we are talking about PBL as a method to create more authentic forms of assessment, PBL is not an add-on or fun project tacked on to the end of a unit to measure what students learned. Instead, PBL is the vehicle used to help students learn and assess that learning.

Project-based learning by its very nature allows students more control over the time, place, pace, and path of their learning, which allows students to have more say. Progress through a project will vary, with students moving at different speeds through the parts of a complex and cognitively demanding project. Inquiry is also at the heart of PBL, so students need time to ask questions, surface wonderings, explore, research, reflect, and revise. PBL places students at the center of learning and reinforces the reality that learning is a messy but rewarding process.

PBLWorks, a professional learning organization that focuses exclusively on project-based learning, identifies the seven design elements necessary to achieve gold-standard PBL:

- a challenging problem or question
- sustained inquiry
- authenticity
- student voice and choice
- reflection
- critique and revision
- the creation of a public product[10]

Through the process of working on a dynamic project, students develop rich content knowledge and specific skills, and teachers can assess the public product to measure progress toward stated learning objectives.

But What about the Grades?

We have discussed how you can design authentic, meaningful assessments before, during, and at the end of a learning experience. As much as we wish that grades did not define learning, we recognize that they are still important. Our goal is to share how we can grade assessments in ways that are transparent, competency based, and clearly communicated to students. In traditional classrooms, many students may not be sure why they are receiving particular assessment scores or what those scores reveal about their areas of strength and weakness.

If something is important enough to grade, and that grade is going in a grade book, students deserve to understand why they are getting the scores they are getting. This can help them develop a higher level of awareness about their strengths as students, as well as identify areas they need to further develop. Assessments should strive to create that clarity for students.

No Gotcha Grades

Catlin

The game of gotcha I associated with assessment growing up made me feel like my teachers did not actually want me to be successful. It was frustrating and defeating. I worked hard and wanted to succeed. Instead of feeling like my teachers were my allies, they felt more like adversaries when it came time for assessments. They asked questions that seemed trivial and irrelevant or deducted points for seemingly arbitrary reasons. There was never an opportunity for me to talk to my teachers about my assessment scores unless I was brave enough to stay after class. I felt like a passive receiver of grades. I had no agency in the grading process. It was a powerless position to be in as a learner. Our learners deserve so much better.

Assessment with Learners

Margaret Heritage, an educational consultant and internationally recognized expert in formative assessment, points out that "the word 'assessment' comes from the Latin verb 'assidere,' meaning 'to sit with.'"[11] This etymology implies that in assessment the teacher sits with the learner, and assessment is something that teachers do with and for students rather than to students. *Balance with Blended Learning* discusses the value of assessing student work with the learner sitting right next to you.[12]

The beauty of a side-by-side assessment is that it creates much-needed transparency around the grading process. You can make your thought process explicit by conducting a think-aloud as you assess a student's work. Ideally, you are using a standards-aligned rubric that targets the specific standards you identified at the start of the design process. That way you can circle language on the rubric as you conduct your think-aloud so students understand why they are receiving specific assessment scores.

It's also important to keep the scope of an assessment narrow and limit the number of criteria being evaluated to avoid overwhelming you and the learner. Many teachers try to assess every aspect of every assignment, which is time-consuming for us and hard for students to process. We encourage a more focused approach where you focus on two or three standards or skills in the assessment. At the end of each side-by-side assessment, ask the student, "Do you have any questions? Is anything unclear?"

Not only does this approach create more transparency and help students to better understand where they are succeeding and where they are struggling, it also creates space for the learner to ask questions or request additional support. These questions and requests can help you to design follow-up learning activities that support individual learner progress.

This approach to assessment takes time, but it is time well spent because it helps us nurture and develop our relationships with students. Side-by-side assessments provide us with data we can use to move toward personalized learning because we have a clearer picture of what each student needs. It also lightens our loads because we won't be spending our evenings and weekends grading summative assessments. By leveraging various blended learning models to shift control over learning to students, teachers also create time and space to pull assessment into the classroom.

SUMMARIZE, REFLECT, AND DISCUSS

Assessment should be woven into the fabric of our work with students—before, during, and at the end of the learning cycle. Effective assessment begins with a clear understanding of the target standards, learning objectives, and the firm goals driving our work. Pre-assessment, or diagnostic, helps us to understand and appreciate the diversity of experience and skills in our class. This data can also help teachers select specific blended learning models to use to reach specific goals.

During the learning, formative assessment data will help teachers and students monitor individual student progress toward learning goals and make the necessary adjustments to personalize a learner's path. Summative assessments are designed to measure progress toward learning objectives and should strive to provide students with flexible means, giving them some choice in terms of how they demonstrate their learning, which is easier to accomplish if teachers explore alternatives to traditional forms of assessment.

Finally, teachers can create some much-needed transparency around the grading process and nurture their relationships with learners if they pull assessment into the classroom and make student progress an ongoing conversation.

- How do you currently use diagnostic, formative, and summative assessments in your learning environment? How might you shift your practice after reading this chapter?

- Choice boards can be brilliant ways to provide multiple means of action and expression, but they have the potential to focus students on different standards, goals, and outcomes. If someone were to ask for advice in creating a universally designed choice board, what would you tell them? Consider making a list of tips!

- The Santiago puppet project was an example of a one-size-fits-all project. Make a list of your one-size-fits-all projects. Next, identify alternative, more authentic ways that students could share how they met the goal of the lesson.

- Consider the value of side-by-side assessments. How might you lean on blended learning models to make time to assess student work with learners? What impact might this practice have on your work load and your students' motivation? How might your approach to grading need to shift to make this a sustainable practice?

CHAPTER 8

Solitude and Communities of Practice

We're Not in Walden Anymore

Katie

Walden Pond is tucked into the woods in Concord, Massachusetts. In the summer, you can swim across the pond, alongside the twisting and tangling of lily pads. In the fall, you can walk around the perimeter, the crackling of sherbet-colored leaves under your boots. The pond, although quiet and serene, is highly trafficked throughout the year, thanks to its importance to the transcendentalist movements of the nineteenth century.

The pond was made famous by Henry David Thoreau, a literary titan of his time. One of his most famous works, *Walden*, chronicled his time when he moved to a one-room shack on the edge of the pond to live in solitude. In the first line of *Walden*, Thoreau wrote, "I went to the woods because I wished to live deliberately." Clearly, the man valued his solitude and silence. He wanted to go it alone.

This essay has become a beacon of sorts, to writers and thinkers who come from around the world to sit by Walden Pond, balance on the abutting railroad tracks, and lean against the same trees that Thoreau may have leaned up against as he contemplated the value of self-reliance and seclusion.

The thing is, Henry David Thoreau did not live in solitude—at least not in the way many people think. His one-room shack was more of a getaway, half a mile from the railroad tracks and the main road in Concord. It was like his man cave, a place where he knew he would be less distracted as he immersed himself in writing. But Thoreau was incredibly social and valued relationships.

The myth that Thoreau was a hermit who lived in solitude is so oft-repeated that it is addressed by the Thoreau Institute at Walden Woods on their website. The project shares that Thoreau made frequent visits to town to see his besties and family, chatted it up with passersby in the woods, and even threw parties at his little shack. Apparently, his annual melon party was off the hook.

Here's the thing: Thoreau valued his autonomy, but he also "highly valued community and maintained close friendships throughout his life."[1] In many ways, teaching and designing a curriculum is a little like Thoreau's *Walden* experiment. All too often, planning is done in solitude, in between classes, up late at night while watching reruns of *Seinfeld,* or on the weekends when, let's face it, you'd rather be attending a kickin' melon party.

But just as Thoreau made time to connect with his community, to co-create experiences, and to continue to build relationships with those around him, we challenge you, through design, to do the same.

Universally Designing Professional Relationships

Universal Design for Learning (UDL) recognizes that teaching, at its core, is emotional work. And emotional work can take an incredible toll on us. Too often, we shoulder much of the work alone, taking in prepping, planning, and assessing in solitude. There is an incredible opportunity, however, to connect with our colleagues. *Innovate Inside the Box*, a book Katie wrote with George Couros, explores how the core of teaching and learning is built on relationships. Taking the time to build and maintain relationships with our colleagues is critical for learning, innovation, and change. At the core of every learning experience is that recognition that every single day, we have an opportunity to create a space where our colleagues feel welcomed and valued. And when we feel welcomed and valued, we are more engaged and learn more.

UDL isn't a framework you can implement overnight and building collegial relationships takes time, patience, and continued practice. Even the most experienced teachers can sometimes struggle with building meaningful relationships with colleagues, so it is critical to foster collaboration and community and a shared responsibility for implementing the UDL framework in a blended learning environment.

As instructional leaders, administrators have an amazing opportunity to model universally designed learning experiences to empower staff and foster collaboration and community. When working with districts, we are often asked, "How do we begin to shift the culture toward building relationships and elevating and celebrating the voices of learners?" As a first step, model UDL with your colleagues, empower their voices, and create engaging opportunities for them to experience high-quality, flexible learning. There are numerous ways to build meaningful connections through professional learning.

Joni Degner, a nationally recognized UDL consultant, wrote an article for EdWeek where she shared how to create a school culture that values relationships and learner identity. Although she wrote the tips for fostering relationships with students, they can be easily adapted for collegial relationships:

- Find regular opportunities for colleagues to co-design professional learning, faculty meetings, and social gatherings.
- Provide opportunities for colleagues to tell their personal stories. As much as it challenges our minds, it also challenges our hearts and is deeply personal work. We need spaces to connect on a personal level, tell stories, and recognize our humanity.
- Provide frequent opportunities to share feedback. In order to build relationships and design better learning experiences, we have to listen. Truly listen. And through this listening, we build empathy. Carving out time for listening and feedback is critical.[2]

To be clear, you don't have to be besties with everyone you work with, but collaboration, community, and work relationships can significantly impact your performance, engagement, collective teacher efficacy, and job satisfaction. Research is clear that positive, authentic relationships with colleagues and administrators result in higher commitment, lower levels of reported job stress, and higher levels of trust, respect, support, and encouragement.[3]

Clearly, if you're alone in your one-room school or you're isolated from your colleagues, you don't get all those benefits. So, how do you build and, more importantly, maintain these relationships through communities of practice (CoP), especially in a flexible learning landscape?

Having close relationships with your colleagues is critical for school culture, but it's bigger than that. It's important to nurture social relationships, but also your cognitive relationships through meaningful co-planning, evidence-based decision making, and professional learning. One strategy educators can use to prioritize their own learning while also developing their relationships with their colleagues is to form a community of practice.

Develop a Community of Practice with Your Peers

A community of practice (CoP) is composed of individuals who share a common concern, set of problems, or a deep passion for a topic, subject, or issue. The goal of participating in a CoP is to deepen and extend your learning by engaging with other people in a process of collective learning. A CoP has three characteristics that set it apart from other types of groups: a) a shared domain of interest, b) a community composed of members with strong relationships, and c) a shared practice aimed at developing resources and building knowledge.[4]

A SHARED DOMAIN OF INTEREST. You may form a CoP with other educators who want to develop expertise in a specific area, like increasing access and equity using the principles of Universal Design for Learning or prioritizing student agency with blended learning models. The shared interest serves to focus and frame the group's energy and learning.

A COMMUNITY COMPOSED OF MEMBERS WITH STRONG RELA-TIONSHIPS. Nurturing the community is key to the health of a CoP. Despite having a million things to do on any given day, it's important to nurture our relationships with colleagues. Those relationships can have a positive impact on teacher engagement at work and help us to feel like we are part of a larger community. Even though many teachers work in close proximity to their colleagues, it's rare to have opportunities to chat, share best practices, or drop in on another teacher's class to observe and learn. Yet these conversations and interactions with your colleagues can lift you up on a tough day, inspire you to try a new strategy or tool, and challenge you to see a situation from a different perspective.

A SHARED PRACTICE AIMED AT DEVELOPING RESOURCES AND BUILDING KNOWLEDGE. A CoP is composed of practitioners interested in developing their skills and knowledge. They are focused on building a repository of resources through conversation, storytelling, and engagement with the other members of the CoP. Over time, these interactions yield a deeper understanding of the domain that brought the group together.[5]

To begin a CoP, educators need to identify a shared area of interest, articulate a clear goal for this community, and raise awareness about the existence of the CoP. Once the CoP has been established, educators can use the strategies below to engage in meaningful learning together—in person, online, or via a combination of the two.

HOST A BOOK STUDY. Select a book on a topic related to the shared domain of interest and engage in a book study. Set up a realistic timeline for reading. Since teachers are always short on time, it's important to set realistic expectations for your reading schedule. Limiting the reading to a couple of chapters per month is likely to feel doable for busy educators. Then schedule a consistent time each month to meet and discuss. These conversations can happen on a Sunday morning at a favorite coffee shop, or members can join from the comfort of their own homes via videoconferencing (coffee in hand, of course!).

SCHEDULE A REGULAR LUNCH DATE OR COFFEE. Sharing a meal or meeting for coffee on a regular basis encourages members of a CoP to connect, build relationships, and nurture the community over time. The more connected the members of a CoP feel to the community, the more likely they are to show up for meetings or engage in conversation. Teachers on a campus can meet for a weekly lunch, and those online may want to plan a virtual morning coffee chat on the first Friday of each month.

MAKE TIME TO CHAT. To build knowledge and develop a repository of resources, educators need to regularly engage in conversation about topics of interest. A CoP can identify a topic of particular interest each month, like fostering productive collaboration among students online or exploring strategies for communicating more effectively with families. Then the group can discuss this topic, sharing useful resources and experiences, to help the members of the CoP think creatively about the issue and design solutions they can all use to develop in their practice.

For busy educators or those working remotely, these ongoing conversations can take the form of a weekly or monthly Twitter chat or discussion thread hosted on the group's Facebook page. Technology is making it easier than ever before to engage in both synchronous and asynchronous conversations as well as share and archive resources.

CoPs provide educators with an avenue to engage with and learn from one another. A CoP may be composed of educators on your campus or may be a virtual group of teachers who want to engage in social learning focused on a particular topic. The beauty of flexible learning landscapes is that learning—both professional learning for educators and academic learning for students—extends beyond a physical location, making it possible for individuals to connect, engage, share, and learn across time and space.

Teachers on a campus can also learn with and from each other by instituting a practice like "Wednesday walks," which are designed to encourage teachers to get out of their classrooms to see what their colleagues are doing. The goal is to spend fifteen to twenty minutes in another teacher's classroom observing and providing informal feedback. Wednesday walks encourage teachers to take risks, try something new, and stretch instructionally. On Wednesdays, teachers put a note out for any teacher who comes into the room to observe, asking for feedback on specific aspects of the lesson. We have seen schools create a simple feedback form that can be accessed by a QR code or short link. That way, the visiting teacher can provide thoughtful, focused, and meaningful feedback on the part of the lesson they observed. Not only does the visiting teacher get to see strategies and models in practice that may serve to inspire their work, but they are also providing feedback to support their colleagues in continued growth.

The most successful and adaptable schools have found ways to build professional learning into the very fabric of the school day and leverage the talented educators on their campuses.

SUMMARIZE, REFLECT, AND DISCUSS

Teaching and learning begins and ends with relationships. Since teaching is emotional work, it is critical that we design opportunities to nurture relationships with colleagues and our students. When we proactively create opportunities to build connections and foster inclusion, collaboration, and community, we ensure that learning is not an isolated event, but rather one woven into the fabric of the authentic lives we live. Just as Henry David Thoreau valued his solitude, he also recognized the power, energy, and happiness he got from close, meaningful relationships. If we want to create a culture of learning and risk taking, with all its ebbs and flows, we have to ensure we have a network of support even when we run deep into the woods.

- Teaching and learning requires that we foster deep, meaningful relationships with our colleagues and our learners. Set a goal or commitment to elevate and celebrate the relationships you have with your colleagues and students.

- Nurturing the community is key to the health of a community of practice (CoP). What are ways that you have nurtured your CoP? If your CoP needs a little love, what are some concrete strategies in this chapter you could implement?

CHAPTER 9

Zooming into Family and Community Engagement

It's about More than Roosters

Katie

For a long time, one of my favorite books to read to my children was *Zoom* by Istvan Banyai. The book has no words and whimsically manipulates point of view by revealing pictures within pictures as you turn from page to page. What begins as a crimson mountain range is revealed to be the crest of a rooster when you flip the page and zoom out. "Ah, it's a rooster!" my kids would shriek before we zoomed out again to see the rooster is framed by a window with a small boy looking out.

"It's not just a rooster, Mom," the kids would giggle. "It's a whole farm." Soon, the farm is revealed to be a child's playset, which is actually the cover of a magazine. The book continues to zoom farther and farther out until you begin to question if anything is as it seems.

When I think about teaching and learning, I zoom into the students and what an incredible gift it is to serve them. Teaching is an incredible act of love that allows us to change the outcomes of kids through design. But when we think about the true calling of our work, we have to zoom out. It's not only our students we serve, but their families, the communities they live in, and the greater world.

When students struggle, we tend to look inward, at providing targeted intervention, fostering relationships, and thinking about more equitable learning design. These are things we can do directly with our learners. But if we step back, we can appreciate that our kids are a part of a much bigger community that has incredible power to improve academic outcomes. Meaningful school-family partnerships have been associated with higher grades and test scores, better attendance, and more positive behaviors.[1] So as we talk about Universal Design for Learning (UDL) and blended learning, it is critical to discuss how we can support and engage parents and our communities in meaningful opportunities to collaborate.

An important distinction to this work is the difference between involvement and engagement. When I was a teacher, I made incredible efforts to involve parents, which is critical but not sufficient. In addition to involving families and the community, we have to engage them.

As an example, when I taught seventh grade, my colleagues and I scheduled parent connections days. Our intent was to provide numerous opportunities for parents to connect with us and learn more about our interdisciplinary work. We recognized the barriers of a single "Back to School Night," where parents are expected to be available to travel to the school at 7:00 p.m., arrange for childcare, and navigate a complicated schedule where they are shuffled in large groups every six minutes. Such a model excludes parents who work in the evenings, can't arrange for childcare, experience discomfort in educational settings, and/or need language support.

We were committed to creating relationships with our families and involving them in the classrooms, so we scheduled one day each quarter where we invited parents into our classrooms to learn more about how we were supporting their children. To advertise these days, we sent home hard copies, left voicemails, sent reminders via email. Parents could come in the morning, the afternoon, or the evening. We all came into work an hour before homeroom and served coffee. One of us would stay back in our rooms so we could supervise younger children and support our own students with extra help if they came. We made ourselves available again at lunch, and in sessions after school and in the evening. Parents could attend in person, schedule phone calls, or schedule another time that worked better. The model was universally designed in many ways, and I'm incredibly grateful for the opportunities we had to connect with families.

What I recognize now was that we created flexible opportunities for parent involvement but not necessarily parent engagement. Furthermore, we didn't make an effort to connect with the community beyond our parents. In hindsight, I'm wishing that we had invited local religious officials, business owners, community organizations, and members at the senior center. All of these stakeholders offer an incredible opportunity to design learning experiences that are authentic, relevant, and meaningful.

Larry Ferlazzo is an award-winning ELL teacher and writer who emphasizes the importance of educators encouraging parent and community engagement in place of parent and community involvement.[2] Engagement requires stakeholders to take action and contribute to the design of learning. Our team invited parents to listen to us discuss curriculum and instruction but did not invite them to co-design the learning with us. We provided numerous opportunities for families to listen, but the goal of the sessions was for parents to learn—not for us to learn.

Our parent sessions provided a beautiful foundation to build relationships, but they would have been even better if we had facilitated community dialogue and offered two-way communication beyond a question-and-answer session. If you're considering a similar approach, create flexible opportunities for families and community members to share feedback on the learning environment and offer ideas for making the curriculum more culturally relevant and responsive, and ask them to determine opportunities for them to participate in teaching and supporting learners.

At the beginning of each year, I asked my learners to interview an important adult in their life. It could be a parent or other relative, a community member, a coach, a local grocer. The only requirement was it was someone they felt a connection to. If they couldn't identify anyone, we would put our heads together to identify someone in the school community. Their task was to find out what the person was good at. It could have been anything! I had students share stories about business owners, expert knitters, connoisseurs of apple pie, and uncles who were deep-sea fishermen. Tapping into student funds of knowledge was the first part of the activity. The second part was exploring how they could contribute their expertise to the school.

Some of the students got very creative and made videos about how I could get a makeover from a makeup artist aunt, which would make me a better (and prettier!) teacher, while others wrote letters or essays about banking, translation, or jiujitsu. I made a note of their discoveries, and throughout the year, whenever I saw an opportunity for a connection, I made it. When we read *The Old Man and the Sea*, Tim's uncle, a commercial fisherman, shared videos and pictures with the class about what it was like to be a fisherman like on *Deadliest Catch*. Taking the time to involve and engage families and the community is critical to better understanding our learners, creating home-school partnerships, and co-creating learning experiences that reflect the lives of the families we serve.

Barriers to Family and Community Engagement

If our goal is to engage families and the communities in meaningful opportunities to collaborate, we have to be aware of the barriers that may derail our critical work. Research has identified three barriers that impact school engagement, especially in communities that have been historically marginalized: silent divide, limited responsiveness, and institutional barriers.[3]

SILENT DIVIDE. Parents and community members sometimes feel that their voices are not heard, or that their voices are not welcome in the school community. One way to minimize this barrier is to provide multiple opportunities for families to share their voices and perspectives in ways that are relevant, authentic, and meaningful. For example, you could schedule blended family connections days! Just as schools are offering learners more options about how they engage—in class or online—we should do the same for parents. We can host chats online, invite parents to record a video, or encourage them to come to campus to connect. Or you may provide a survey tool in multiple languages and provide hard copies, links to online surveys, or opportunities to join community dialogues where parents and community members can share how they would like to collaborate with schools or their ideas for how schools can better serve learners. Once you get the results, reflect on them and share how they will impact your practice.

Family voices are essential. In the spring of 2020, when learning went remote because of COVID-19, there were a number of educators who began posting something along the lines of "If you're not currently teaching, you don't get a say in how I'm doing" online. Certainly, we understand how overwhelmed educators were and how hard everyone was working. But when we serve people's babies, those families get a voice. As practitioners, not only do we need to find ways to involve parents, we need to create opportunities for two-way communication and for parents and community members to share what they need to better support our kids.

LIMITED RESPONSIVENESS. Some family and community members feel that schools and districts aren't responsive to the authentic needs of the families they serve. "Open House" or "Back to School Night" are examples of limited responsiveness. In a study on family and community engagement, a parent noted that schools were often unresponsive to the needs of parents. She shared, "I know they have . . . parent council meetings . . . but it's from five to six. It's kind of hard if you do work."[4] Engaging families means being available outside of traditional involvement sessions, and with blended learning, there are incredible opportunities to create asynchronous opportunities for families to not only be involved but to be engaged.

INSTITUTIONAL BARRIERS. Many teachers are incredibly responsive to parents, but even when individual teachers create flexible pathways for parent engagement, there are many procedures and policies that restrict teachers from implementing suggestions. One parent in the study noted, "Of course, I mean everything is data-driven; it's not their fault. I don't blame [administrators] personally; I just blame the institution."

The institutional barriers remind us, again, that we have to zoom out and look at a bigger picture. If you are a classroom teacher, or a school-based leader, you have numerous opportunities to create flexible pathways for parents and community members to share their voices and contribute to positive change, but you still may face barriers at the institutional level. Despite this reality, you still have the power to allow families and the community to be heard. It is true that a single person cannot change the system or the institution of education today. But remember there is always so much you can, in fact, change. In your classroom or in your school, you can close the silent divide and be more responsive to the needs of your families by creating flexible, blended opportunities for involvement and engagement.

Basketball Glory Days

Katie

I was a good basketball player back in the day. Because I hit -five eight in fifth grade, I was the perfect center, or the "big man," on the court. The problem was, I never got any taller. I couldn't change that on the court. Sure, I can wear high heels now, but they aren't super helpful if I'm trying to box out an opponent. Here's the thing: I could have focused on the fact that I was up against girls six feet and taller, or I could work on my game at five eight. I worked on my vertical jump, worked on getting quicker, and learned to read the body language of opponents. The first lady to the ball gets the ball. By focusing on what I could alter, I could own the boards. For the remainder of this chapter, we're going to zoom back to look at what you can control with parent and community engagement, and then use the UDL lens and blended learning to ensure that it is accessible, authentic, and linguistically appropriate.

Shifting the Focus from What Families Don't Have to What They Do

Zaretta Hammond, an expert on culturally responsive pedagogy, encourages educators to shift their focus from what families or students don't have to what they *do* have. In an episode of the podcast *Vrain Waves*, she compares the challenges presented by distance learning with the events in the movie *Apollo 13*.[5] When the astronauts announced, "Houston, we have a problem," the team on the ground launched into action. They had a box containing all the items the astronauts had access to in their spacecraft. They used that box of items to design a solution that the team in space could replicate to deal with the damage caused by the explosion. Hammond says that's how we have to approach our work when students and parents are navigating online learning. She says, "We cannot replicate the school day at home, and we shouldn't try." We couldn't agree more.

Each learning landscape offers unique affordances. Instead of attempting to re-create a face-to-face learning experience when students are learning remotely, we have to reimagine our approach to capitalize on what students have access to at home. We have to understand what our students and their families have in their *Apollo 13* box.

- What resources are available to learners?
- Do they have a backyard or front porch where they can make and document observations?
- Is there someone at home who can accompany the learner on a walk around the neighborhood to engage in fieldwork or collect data?
- Is there a space where students can do a cooking project that focuses on measurement and following directions?
- Does the student have someone at home they can engage in conversation with to surface their learning?
- Do they have access to recycled items, like cardboard, for projects and assignments?
- Do they have a device they can use to take pictures or record short videos?

All of these are important questions to ask if we are going to design learning experiences that are accessible as learners work from home. This means we have to find ways to connect and communicate with families.

If we find out what students have access to, we can design learning experiences to remove barriers and capitalize on those resources. If there are items that students absolutely need to complete a particular task that they do not currently have, we have to ask how we can get those supplies to students.

Magic of Materials Pickup

Catlin

During the school closures in spring and fall of 2020, my children's school hosted a monthly materials pickup. They provided a list of items to be included in the pickup and offered several windows of time when families could drive up, masks on, and receive a bag of goodies. My son was enrolled in a STEM elective, so his bag contained wire, popsicle sticks, and Styrofoam. They also had bags with hot glue guns and glue sticks, rolls of tape, and scissors for families who needed them. This random assortment of items, many of which we did not have at home, made it possible for my son to design and build a crankshaft. This hands-on project was one of his favorites because it provided a much-needed break from the screen.

Parents as Partners

When our kids were in the early elementary grades, teachers were quick to ask for help. They were always looking for "parent volunteers." We both spent many afternoons in our children's kindergarten and first-grade classrooms working with small groups of students, preparing materials for art projects, and helping to mark papers. We enjoyed being helpful and knew our kids' teachers had their hands full with a room of tiny humans.

As our kids grow older, the requests are fewer and farther between. Since no one requests volunteers at Back to School Night, we spend less and less time in our kids' schools and classrooms.

Hammond makes the important point that "parents have always been the students' first teachers."[6] Parents are natural teachers. They teach students how to stack blocks, share items with siblings, say their first words, and tie their shoes. These are things we do as parents without any formal training, so can you imagine how effective parents could be with support? How much more successful could students be learning online if we recorded videos to provide step-by-step directions, how-to tutorials, and models of strategies for parents? Since parents, guardians, and caregivers are essentially learning coaches when students are learning remotely, we should consider how we can support their work from a distance and empower them with the resources and tools necessary to support their learners.

A partnership with our students' families, just like our partnership with learners, requires mutual trust and respect, combined with open, honest communication. It isn't about talking *at* families and telling them what we are doing. Instead the goal should be to provide windows into the wonderful work their children are doing, tap into the parents' or guardians' funds of knowledge and expertise, and co-construct learning with them. You can begin to do this by implementing the following strategies:

PROVIDE WINDOWS INTO THE WORK. Document what is happening in the classroom by taking photos, recording videos, and saving examples of student work. Then share this documentation of the learning with parents. Teachers can use digital or print newsletters, send email updates, start a YouTube channel for parents, or post weekly updates to a class blog that parents can access from any device. If parents know what kids are working on, they are more

likely to offer support. Consider the following questions as you create the correspondence you plan to share with families.

- Why are we doing what we're doing?
- What are the learning objectives of a unit or learning cycle?
- What key concepts, vocabulary words, or skills will we be
  focusing on? How will we work toward mastering those
  concepts, words, or skills?
- What assignments or projects are they working on? What
  supplies or assistance will students need or benefit from?
- How can parents support their students at home? Can they
  engage their child in conversation using a set of questions or
  review a list of vocabulary words with them?
- What type of parent or community support or assistance
  would be helpful during a unit or learning cycle?

Breaking up the text with visuals that allow families to "see" what
kids are working on or creating is more engaging than a lengthy
multiparagraph correspondence. Using video may also allow these
updates to be more accessible. Even if you are recording your video
update in English, you can add closed captioning in different languages to make the video accessible for families that speak another
language at home.

**TAP INTO PARENTS' AND GUARDIANS' FUNDS OF KNOWLEDGE
AND EXPERTISE.** Tap into the parent population and the larger
community to supplement the learning, making it richer and more
dynamic. Think of every individual like a square of fabric—the kind
you might see in a bin at the fabric store. Each square has its own colors and patterns, but when sewn together, they create these beautiful
and unique quilts.

Imagine students are reading *The Omnivore's Dilemma*. You have
an incredible opportunity to send out requests to parents, families,
staff, the school board, the district office, and local community

groups asking for volunteers to come in and speak with students about farming, food production, nutrition, etc. You will be flooded with expertise and amazed by the wealth of knowledge in your community and how willing people are to spend time with your students.

Imagine how much richer the lessons would be if you had a mushroom expert come in to talk about the healing properties of mushrooms. You could host a panel of family and community members who have experience working on local farms and ask them to come in to answer questions about the realities of working on a farm. You could organize a field trip to the local farmers' market or community garden so students could interview the people growing or selling their produce and items. A nutritionist and trainer could come in to talk to students about diet, exercise, and how the body functions.

CO-CONSTRUCT LEARNING EXPERIENCES. When students are learning online, we are likely to have more success engaging them if we work with parents to design learning experiences that are accessible and interesting. Parents, guardians, and caregivers are the ones with the best insight into what their students are enjoying, what they are struggling with, and what modifications may improve their experience. Asking parents to share feedback or join a monthly videoconference call can help us to better understand what is working and what is not working. Just as collecting feedback from students provides invaluable insight into their experience, asking parents for feedback can do the same. Additionally, if we communicate what we plan to do ahead of time, we can collect feedback and suggestions from families, which allows us to create learning that reflects the lived experiences of our learners and their families.

SUMMARIZE, REFLECT, AND DISCUSS

So much of the work in our schools is focused on our students, as it should be. But if we zoom back, we can see the incredible potential to co-serve these learners by collaborating with their families and the community. Every day, families trust our schools and our teachers enough to share their babies with us. Making time for meaningful involvement and collaboration with them is not just another thing we have to do. Rather, it's a critical component of our work.

- Family and community engagement requires us to design opportunities for both involvement and engagement. After reading this chapter, what strategies could you implement to foster family and community engagement in your learning environment?
- It's critical that we have an asset-based mindset when collaborating with families. When you think about your families and their funds of knowledge, what do they have in their *Apollo 13* box?
- Blended learning may include at-home learning. How can you collaborate with parents to design learning experiences that are accessible as learners work from home?

Conclusion

In the book *The Alchemist*, by Paulo Coelho, a young boy is traveling around the world, seeking the meaning of life.[1] He is unsure about his path and his next steps and looks for direction from people he meets on his journey. In one scene, he meets a wise man who reminds him to look inward. He hands the boy a spoon filled with precious oil. He tells the boy to wander around the grounds of the property without allowing the oil to spill.

When the boy returns, the wise man welcomes him back and asks, "Did you see the Persian tapestries that are hanging in my dining hall? Did you see the garden that it took the master gardener ten years to create? Did you notice the beautiful parchments in the library?" The boy was embarrassed and confessed that he had observed nothing. His only concern had been not spilling the oil the wise man had entrusted to him.

"Then go back and observe the marvels of the world," the wise man said. The boy stepped out and explored, marveling at everything he had missed. Upon returning to the wise man, he related every detail of what he had seen. "But where are the drops of oil I entrusted to you?" asked the wise man. Looking down at the spoon he held, the boy saw the oil was gone.

"Well, there is only one piece of advice I can give you. The secret is to see all the marvels of the world and never forget the drops of oil in the spoon."

We share this story because we imagine you picked up this book and took this journey with us because you want to better meet the needs of your learners. You are working incredibly hard and yet not all students are engaged in expert learning. You plan lessons for one learning landscape only to have that landscape unexpectedly shift. You are working harder than your students, and you know there has to be another way. Universally designed blended learning is the way. That being said, we want to remind you not to forget the oil in the spoon.

You don't need to abandon all your current practices to implement universally designed blended learning. Although we have provided guidance, examples, and strategies, you do not have to implement them all at once. Think big, but start small. You have practices that are working for you and your learners. Don't let them go. Instead, consider the barriers that students may face and incorporate strategies that will transfer decision-making to them. You can make the strategies you've used with success in the past even better and more accessible for all learners by using what you've learned about UDL and blended learning.

As your practice shifts, you will begin to see students become expert learners, and you will also have more opportunities to provide feedback, intervention, and enrichment to flexible groups. By designing teaching and learning through the lens of UDL and blended learning, not only are you creating pathways for students to be more effective learners, you will also create a model that allows you to be a more effective teacher. You'll find you have more opportunities to connect with learners in a meaningful and authentic way. You will have *more* time to implement your most effective strategies to targeted groups of learners, which will help you to build relationships with learners while increasing student engagement and improving learning outcomes. And the best part of implementing both UDL and blended learning is that the design will work in any learning landscape.

Let's face it. Learner variability and technology are here to stay, so embracing UDL and blended learning provide solid complementary frameworks to guide teachers in designing and facilitating learning in-class, online, or a beautiful blend of the two! Just like the duck boat, your versatile skill set paired with a new mindset and toolset can help you successfully navigate any terrain with confidence.

Given the variability of the readers of this text, there is not a single strategy that will work for all of you. Throughout this text, we've provided some tips to get started, but look inward, and think about which of the options and choices is best for you. And then, take the next step.

As you grow in your practice as an expert learner, embrace perseverance, a growth mindset, and the value of consistent reflection and change. There is no ceiling, no 100 percent, no A+ when it comes to being a teacher. Expert learning is a lifetime commitment and cannot flourish if we don't try new strategies, reflect on success, and course correct. The best teachers are those who passionately pursue their own learning and, in turn, share that passion with students. We hope you use what you have learned reading this book to experiment, fail forward, iterate, and grow. Your students will benefit from your work as an expert learner.

And think of us being with you every step of the way, whether you journey by water, by land, by foot, or by boat. Where you begin is not as important as where your journey takes you.

Endnotes

INTRODUCTION

1 Margaret Wang, Geneva Haertel, and Herbert Walberg, "The Effectiveness of Collaborative School-Linked Services," National Research Center on Education in the Inner Cities 93(5e), 1993.

2 Alanna Bjorklund-Young and Jay Stratte Plasman, "Reducing the Achievement Gap: Middle Grades Mathematics Performance and Improvement," *Research in Middle Level Education Online* 43, no. 10 (2020), 25–45.

3 Ethan Yazzie-Mintz, *Charting the Path from Engagement to Achievement: A Report on the 2009 High School Survey of Student Engagement* (Bloomington, IN: Center for Evaluation and Education Policy, 2009).

4 Simon Sinek, *Start with Why* (London Penguin Books, 2011).

5 Ki Sung, "What the Shortcomings of EdTech Mean for Improving Distance Learning and Schools," *Mindshift,* September 25, 2020, kqed.org/mindshift.

CHAPTER 1

1 Center for Universal Design, *The Principles of Universal Design,* 1997.

2 Anne Meyer, David Rose, and David Gordon, *Universal Design for Learning: Theory and Practice* (Wakefield, MA: CAST Professional Publishing, 2014), 20.

3 H.R. 4137—110th Congress: "Higher Education Opportunity Act." GovTrack.us. 2007. Accessed May 19, 2021, govtrack.us/congress/bills/110/hr4137.

4 Heather Staker and Michael Horn, *Classifying K-12 Blended Learning* (Mountain View, CA: Innosight Institute, 2012).

5 Susan Patrick, Kathryn Kennedy, and Allison Powell, *Mean What You Say: Defining and Integrating Personalized, Blended and Competency Education* (Vienna, VA: International Association for K–12 Online Learning, 2013), 10.

6 Staker and Horn, *Classifying K-12 Blended Learning.*

7 Staker and Horn, *Classifying K-12 Blended Learning.*

8   Catlin Tucker, Tiffany Wycoff, and Jason Green, *Blended Learning in Action: A Practical Guide toward Sustainable Change* (Thousand Oaks, CA: Sage Publications, 2017).

9   Guy Roth, Avi Assor, Yaniv Kanat-Maymon, and Haya Kaplan, "Autonomous Motivation for Teaching: How Self-Determined Teaching May Lead to Self-Determined Learning," *Journal of Educational Psychology* 99, no. 4 (2007): 761.

10 Phillip Schlechty, *Engaging Students: The Next Level of Working on the Work* (San Francisco: Jossey-Bass, 2011).

11 udlguidelines.cast.org.

12 Kavita Rao and Grace Meo, "Using Universal Design for Learning to Design Standards-Based Lessons," *SAGE Open* 6, no. 4 (2016).

13 John Dewey, *How We Think* (Boston: D.C. Heath & Co., 1910).

14 Katie Novak and Kristan Rodriguez, *UDL Progression Rubric* (CAST Professional Publishing, 2018).

15 Carol Tomlinson, *The Differentiated Classroom: Responding to the Needs of All Learners* (Alexandria, VA: ASCD, 2000).

CHAPTER 2

1   Jennifer Gonsalvez, "Frickin packets," Cult of Pedagogy, last modified March 26, 2018, cultofpedagogy.com/busysheets.

2   Boris Kabanoff, "Equity, Equality, Power, and Conflict," *Academy of Management Review* 16 (1991): 416.

3   Kabanoff, "Equity, Equality, Power, and Conflict."

4   The New Teacher Project (TNTP), "The Opportunity Myth: What Students Can Show Us about How School Is Letting Them Down—and How to Fix It," opportunitymyth.tntp.org/.

5   Chris Emdin, "Reality Pedagogy," *TEDx Talks,* last modified August 23, 2012, youtube.com/watch?v=2Y9tVf_8fqo.

6   Amber Valdez, Sola Takahashi, Kelsey Krausen, Alicia Bowman, and Edith Gurrola, *Getting Better at Getting More Equitable: Opportunities and Barriers for Using Continuous Improvement to Advance Educational Equity*, WestEd, 2020.

7   d.School at Stanford University, *Design Thinking Bootleg*, accessed March 8, 2021, dschool.stanford.edu/resources/design-thinking-bootleg, 4.

8   George Couros, *The Innovator's Mindset* (San Diego, CA: Dave Burgess Consulting, 2015), 49.

9   d.School at Stanford University, *Design Thinking Bootleg,* 15.

10 Mirko Chardin and Katie Novak, *Equity by Design: Delivering on the Power and Promise of Universal Design for Learning* (Thousand Oaks: Corwin, 2020), 71.

11 Chris Emdin, *For White Folks Who Teach in the Hood . . . and the Rest of Y'all Too* (Boston: Beacon Press, 2016), 66.

12 Marina Castro, Linda Choi, Joel Knudson and Jennifer O'Day, *Grading Policy in the Time of COVID-19: Considerations and Implications for Equity* (San Mateo, CA: California Collaborative on District Reform, 2020).

13 Alexis Cherewka, "The Digital Divide Hits U.S. Immigrant Households Disproportionately during the COVID-19 Pandemic," *Migration Policy Institute*, September 3, 2020, migrationpolicy.org/article/digital-divide-hits-us-immigrant-households-during-covid-19.

14 Hailly Korman, Bonnie O'Keefe, and Matt Repka, "Missing in the Margins: Estimating the Scale of the COVID-19 Attendance Crisis," last modified October 21, 2020, bellwethereducation.org/publication/missing-margins-estimating-scale-covid-19-attendance-crisis.

15 Korman, O'Keefe, and Repka, "Missing in the Margins."

16 BethAnn Berliner, Vanessa Barrat, Anthony Fong, and Paul Shirk, "Reenrollment of High School Dropouts in a Large, Urban School District," *Issues & Answers Report*, REL 2008, no. 56 (2008).

17 Future Ready Schools, "16.9 Million Children Remain Logged Out Because They Don't Have Internet at Home," accessed March 8, 2021, futureready.org/homework-gap.

18 Future Ready Schools, "16.9 Million Children."

19 Pedro Noguera, "Where the Promise of the American Dream Falls Short in Schools," *Edutopia,* last modified December 11, 2020, edutopia.org/video/where-promise-american-dream-falls-short-schools.

20 Allison Powell, Beth Rabbit, and Kathryn Kennedy, *iNACOL Blended Learning Teacher Competency Framework* (Vienna, VA: International Association for K-12 Online Learning, 2014), 9.

21 Cecilia Rios-Aguilar, Judy Marquez Kiyama, Michael Gravitt, and Luis C. Moll, "Funds of Knowledge for the Poor and Forms of Capital for the Rich? A Capital Approach to Examining Funds of Knowledge," *Theory and Research in Education* 9, no. 2 (2011): 163–184.

22 Luis C. Moll, Cathy Amanti, Deborah Neff, and Norma Gonzalez, "Funds of Knowledge for Teaching: Using a Qualitative Approach to Connect Homes and Classrooms," *Theory into Practice* 31, no. 2 (1992): 132–141.

CHAPTER 3

1 Kimberly Chrisman Campbell, "The Height of Fashion," Getty, last modified July 26, 2015, blogs.getty.edu/iris/the-height-of-fashion/.

2 "Enterprise Design Field Guide," IBM, accessed March 8, 2021, ibm.com/cloud/architecture/files/design-thinking-field-guide.pdf.

3 Rao and Meo, "Using Universal Design."

4 Katie Novak, "UDL Flowchart," Novak Consulting, accessed May 1, 2021, novakeducation.com/hubfs/Resources/UDL_FlowChart.pdf.

5   Patrick, Kennedy, and Powell, *Mean What You Say.*

6   Fatih Koca, "Motivation to Learn and Teacher–Student Relationship," *Journal of International Education and Leadership* 6, no. 2 (2016).

7   Tucker, *Balance with Blended Learning: Partner with Your Students to Reimagine Learning and Reclaim Your Life* (Thousand Oaks, CA: Corwin Press, 2020).

8   Engage NY, "Grade 3 Eureka Math, Module 4, Lesson 11," last accessed March 15, 2021, engageny.org/resource/grade-3-mathematics-module-4-topic-c-lesson-11/file/35171.

9   youtube.com/watch?v=zUylkrPSpzM.

CHAPTER 4

1   Andrew Mattarella-Micke and Sian Beilock, "Individual Differences in Working Memory: Implications for Learning and Performance," *Encyclopedia of the Sciences of Learning* (Boston: Springer, 2012).

2   Anita Archer and Charles Hughes, *Explicit Instruction: Effective and Efficient Teaching* (New York: Guilford Press, 2011), 18.

3   Andrew Tawfik, Woei Hung, and Phillipe Giabbeanelli, "Comparing Different Inquiry-Based Approaches," *Interdisciplinary Journal of Problem-based Learning*, 14, no.1 (2020).

4   Anita Archer and Charles Hughes, *Explicit Instruction: Effective and Efficient Teaching.*

5   Thomas Thibodeau, "UDL, Online Accessibility, and Virtual Reality: Designing Accessible and Engaging Online Courses," in *Transforming Higher Education through Universal Design for Learning* (London: Routledge, Taylor and Francis Group, 2019).

6   Philip J. Guo, Juho Kim, and Rob Rubin, "How Video Production Affects Student Engagement: An Empirical Study of MOOC Videos," March, 2014, researchgate.net/publication/262393281_How_video_production_affects_student_engagement_An_empirical_study_of_MOOC_videos.

7   Guo, Kim and Rubin, "How Video Production Affects Student Engagement," 44.

8   Cynthia Brame, "Effective Educational Videos," Vanderbilt University Center for Teaching, accessed March 8, 2021, cft.vanderbilt.edu/guides-sub-pages/effective-educational-video.

9   Ben Kalb and Rebecca Peters, interview with Zaretta Hammond, *Vrain Waves*, podcast, May 12, 2020, blogs.svvsd.org/vrainwaves/transcript-episode-056-apollo-13ing-it-with-zaretta-hammond.

CHAPTER 5

1   Steven Bodio and Arthur Shilstone, "Pigeon Racing: Homing in on an 'Invisible' Sport," *Smithsonian* 21 (1990).

2   Joseph Mcdonald, Nancy Mohr, Alan Dichter, and Elaine McDonald, *The Power of Protocols: An Educator's Guide to Improving Practice*, 3rd ed. (New York: Teachers College Press, 2013).

3   Catherine Ennis and M. Terri McCauley, "Creating Urban Classroom Communities Worthy of Trust," *Journal of Curriculum Studies* 34, no. 2 (2002): 169.

4   Catherine Ennis and M. Terri McCauley, "Creating Urban Classroom Communities Worthy of Trust," *Journal of Curriculum Studies* 34, no. 2 (2002): 169.

5   Catlin Tucker, *Balance with Blended learning: Partner with Your Students to Reimagine Learning and Reclaim Your Life* (Thousand Oaks, CA: Sage Publications, 2020).

6   Michael Henderson and Michael Phillips, "Video-Based Feedback on Student Assessment: Scarily Personal," *Australasian Journal of Educational Technology* 31, no. 1 (2015).

7   Karim Shabani, Mohamad Khatib, and Saman Ebadi, "Vygotsky's Zone of Proximal Development: Instructional Implications and Teachers' Professional Development," *English Language Teaching* 3, no. 4 (2010).

8   D. Randy Garrison, Terry Anderson, and Walter Archer, "Critical Inquiry in a Text-Based Environment: Computer Conferencing in Higher Education," *The Internet and Higher Education*, 2 (1999).

9   Zehra Akyol and D. Randy Garrison, "Understanding Cognitive Presence in an Online and Blended Community Of Inquiry: Assessing Outcomes and Processes for Deep Approaches to Learning," *British Journal of Educational Technology* 42, no. 2 (2011): 233–250.

10 Karen Swan, "Social Construction of Knowledge and the Community of Inquiry Framework" in *Open and Distance Education Theory Revisited* (Tokyo: Springer Briefs in Education, 2019), 57-65.

11 Alberto Beuchot and Mark Bullen, "Interaction and Interpersonality in Online Discussion Forums," *Distance Education* 26 (2005).

12 Swan, "Social Construction of Knowledge and the Community of Inquiry Framework."

13 Betsy Mikel, "How Brené Brown Runs Emotionally Intelligent Zoom meetings," *Inc.*, accessed March 8, 2021, inc.com/betsy-mikel/how-brene-brown-runs-emotionally-intelligent-zoom-meetings.html.

14 Kelly Matthews, Victoria Andrews, and Peter Adams, "Social Learning Spaces and Student Engagement," *Higher Education Research & Development* 30, no. 2 (2011).

CHAPTER 6

1   "75 years of crosswords," *New York Times*, last modified February 14, 2017, nytimes.com/interactive/2017/02/14/crosswords/new-york-times-crossword-timeline.html.

2   Jaclyn Broadbent, "Comparing Online and Blended Learner's Self-Regulated Learning Strategies and Academic Performance," *The Internet and Higher Education* 33 (2017); Jaclyn Broadbent and Walter Poon, "Self-Regulated Learning Strategies and Academic

Achievement in Online Higher Education Learning Environments: A Systematic Review," *The Internet and Higher Education* 27 (2015): 1–13.

3 Athanasia Chatzipantelia, Vasilis Grammatikopoulos, and Athanasios Gregoriadis, "Development and Evaluation of Metacognition in Early Childhood Education," *Early Child Development and Care* 184 (2014): 1223.

4 Chatzipantelia, Grammatikopoulos, and Gregoriadis, "Development and Evaluation of Metacognition in Early Childhood Education," 1227.

5 Saemah Rahman, Zuria Mahmud, Siti Fatimah Mohd Yassin, Ruslin Amir, and Khadijah Wan Ilias, "The Development of Expert Learners in the Classroom," *Contemporary Issues in Education Research (CIER)* 3, no. 1 (2010).

6 Marylene Gagne and Edward Deci, "Self-Determination Theory and Work Motivation," *Journal of Organizational Behavior* 26 (2005).

7 Fatma Gizem, Karaoglan Yilmaz, and Hafize Keser, "The Impact of Reflective Thinking Activities in E-learning: A Critical Review of the Empirical Research," *Computers & Education* 95 (2016).

CHAPTER 7

1 Kilbane and Milman, *Teaching Models: Designing Instruction for 21st Century Learners* (Hoboken, NJ: Pearson, 2013).

2 Lorna Earl and Steven Katz, *Rethinking Classroom Assessment with Purpose in Mind: Assessment for Learning, Assessment as Learning, Assessment of Learning* (Manitoba, Western and Northern Canadian Protocol for Collaboration in Education, 2006).

3 Anne Meyer, David Rose, and David Gordon, *UDL Theory and Practice,* 2016, 73.

4 Spencer J. Salend, *Creating Inclusive Classrooms: Effective, Differentiated, and Reflective Practices* (Columbus, OH: Pearson Education, 2016).

5 Tucker, *Balance with Blended Learning.*

6 Grant Wiggins and Jay McTighe, *Understanding by Design,* 2nd edition (Alexandria, VA: ASCD, 2005).

7 Kilbane and Milman, *Teaching Models: Designing Instruction for 21st Century Learners.*

8 Jay McTighe, "What is a performance task?" Defined Learning, last modified April 10, 2015, blog.performancetask.com/what-is-a -performance-task-part-1-9fa0d99ead3b.

9 "What is PBL?" Buck Institute for Education, last accessed March 8, 2021, pblworks.org/what-is-pbl.

10 "What is PBL?" Buck Institute for Education.

11 Margaret Heritage, *Formative Assessment: Making It Happen in the Classroom* (Thousand Oaks, CA: Corwin Press, 2010).

12 Tucker, *Balance with Blended Learning.*

CHAPTER 8

1 "Myths and Misconceptions," Walden Woods Project, last accessed March 9, 2021, walden.org/education/for-students/ myths-and-misconceptions/.

2 Joni Degner, "How Universal Design for Learning Creates Culturally Accessible Classrooms," *Education Week*, last modified November 15, 2016, edweek.org/education/opinion-how-universal-design -for-learning-creates-culturally-accessible-classrooms/2016/11.

3 Khoa Tran, Phuong Nguyen, Thao Dang, Tran Ton, "The Impacts of the High-Quality Workplace Relationships on Job Performance: A Perspective on Staff Nurses in Vietnam," *Behavioral Sciences* 8, no. 12 (2018): 109.

4 Etienne Wenger, Richard McDermott, and William M. Snyder, *Cultivating Communities of Practice: A Guide to Managing Knowledge* (Cambridge, MA: Harvard Business Press, 2002).

5 Etienne Wenger, "Communities of Practice and Social Learning Systems: The Career of a Concept" in *Social Learning Systems and Communities of Practice* (London: Springer, 2010), 179–198.

CHAPTER 9

1 Amy Cook, Alveena Shah, Lauren Brodsky, and Laura J Morizio, "Strengthening School-Family-Community Engagement through Community Dialogues," *Journal for Social Action in Counseling & Psychology* 9, no. 1 (2017).

2 Larry Ferlazzo, "Involvement or Engagement," *Educational Leadership* 68, no. 8 (2011).

3 Cook, Shah, Brodsky, and Morizio, "Strengthening School-Family-Community Engagement through Community Dialogues."

4 Cook, Shah, Brodsky, and Morizio, "Strengthening School-Family-Community Engagement through Community Dialogues," 17.

5 Ben Kalb and Rebecca Peters, interview with Zaretta Hammond, *Vrain Waves.*

6 Ben Kalb and Rebecca Peters, interview with Zaretta Hammond, *Vrain Waves.*

References

Akyol, Zehra, and Randy Garrison. "Understanding Cognitive Presence in an Online and Blended Community of Inquiry: Assessing Outcomes and Processes for Deep Approaches to Learning." *British Journal of Educational Technology* 42, no. 2 (2011): 233–250.

Archer, Anita, and Charles Hughes. *Explicit Instruction: Effective and Efficient Teaching*. New York: Guilford Press, 2011.

Berliner, BethAnn, Vanessa Barrat, Anthony Fong, and Paul Shirk. "Reenrollment of High School Dropouts in a Large, Urban School District." *Issues & Answers Report,* REL 2008, no. 056 (2008). ies.ed.gov/ncee/edlabs.

Beuchot, Alberto, and Mark Bullen. "Interaction and Interpersonality in Online Discussion Forums." *Distance Education* 26, no. 1 (2005): 67–87.

Bjorklund-Young, Alanna, and Jay Stratte Plasman. "Reducing the Achievement Gap: Middle Grades Mathematics Performance and Improvement." *Research in Middle Level Education Online* 43, no. 10 (2020), 25–45.

Bodio, Steven, and Arthur Shilstone. "Pigeon Racing: Homing in on an 'Invisible' Sport." *Smithsonian* 21, no. 7 (1990): 80.

Brame, Cynthia. "Effective Educational Videos." *Vanderbilt University*. Accessed March 8, 2021. cft.vanderbilt.edu/guides-sub-pages/effective-educational-video.

Broadbent, Jaclyn. "Comparing Online and Blended Learner's Self-Regulated Learning Strategies and Academic Performance." *The Internet and Higher Education* 33 (2017): 24–32.

Broadbent, Jaclyn, and Walter Poon. "Self-Regulated Learning Strategies and Academic Achievement in Online Higher Education Learning Environments: A Systematic Review." *The Internet and Higher Education* 27 (2015): 1–13.

Campbell, Kimberly Chrisman. "The Height of Fashion." Getty. Last modified July 26, 2015. blogs.getty.edu/iris/the-height-of-fashion/.

Castro, Marina, Linda Choi, Joel Knudson, and Jennifer O'Day. *Grading Policy in the Time of COVID-19: Considerations and Implications for Equity.* San Mateo, CA: California Collaborative on District Reform, 2020.

Center for Universal Design. "The Principles of Universal Design." Last modified April 1, 1997. projects.ncsu.edu/ncsu/design/cud/about_ud/udprinciplestext.htm.

Chardin, Mirko, and Katie Novak. *Equity by Design. Delivering on the Power and Promise of UDL.* Thousand Oaks, CA: Corwin, 2020.

Chatzipantelia, Athanasia, Vasilis Grammatikopoulos, and Athanasios Gregoriadis. "Development and Evaluation of Metacognition in Early Childhood Education." *Early Child Development and Care* 184, no. 8, (2014): 1223–1232.

Cherewka, Alexis. "The Digital Divide Hits U.S. Immigrant Households Disproportionately during the COVID-19 Pandemic." *Migration Policy Institute.* Last modified September 3, 2020. migrationpolicy.org/article/digital-divide-hits-us-immigrant-households-during-covid-19.

Coelho, Paulo. *The Alchemist.* San Francisco: Harper, 1998.

Cook, Amy, Alveena Shah, Lauren Brodsky, and Laura J Morizio. "Strengthening School-Family-Community Engagement through Community Dialogues." *Journal for Social Action in Counseling & Psychology* 9, no.1 (2017): 1–29.

Couros, George. *The Innovator's Mindset.* San Diego, CA: Dave Burgess Consulting, 2015.

d.School at Stanford University. Design Thinking Bootleg. Accessed March 8, 2021. dschool.stanford.edu/resources/design-thinking-bootleg.

Degner, Joni. "How Universal Design for Learning Creates Culturally Accessible Classrooms." *Education Week.* Last modified November 15, 2016. edweek.org/education/opinion-how-universal-design-for-learning-creates-culturally-accessible-classrooms/2016/11.

Dewey, John. *How We Think.* Boston: D.C. Heath & Co., 1910.

Earl, Lorna, and Steven Katz. *Rethinking Classroom Assessment with Purpose in Mind: Assessment for Learning, Assessment as Learning, Assessment of Learning.* Manitoba: Western and Northern Canadian Protocol for Collaboration in Education, 2006.

Emdin, Chris. "Reality Pedagogy." *TEDx Talks.* Last modified August 23, 2012. youtube.com/watch?v=2Y9tVf_8fqo.

Emdin, Chris. *For White Folks Who Teach in the Hood . . . and the Rest of Y'all Too.* Boston: Beacon Press, 2016.

Ennis, Catherine, and M. Terri McCauley. "Creating Urban Classroom Communities Worthy of Trust." *Journal of Curriculum Studies* 34, no. 2 (2002): 149–172.

Ferlazzo, Larry. "Involvement or Engagement." *Educational Leadership* 68, no. 8 (2011).

Future Ready Schools. "16.9 Million Children Remain Logged out Because They Don't Have Internet at Home." Accessed March 8, 2021. futureready.org/homework-gap.

Gagne, Marylene, and Edward Deci. "Self-Determination Theory and Work Motivation." *Journal of Organizational Behavior* 26 (2005): 331–362.

Garrison, D. Randy, Terry Anderson, and Walter Archer. "Critical Inquiry in a Text-Based Environment: Computer Conferencing in Higher Education." *The Internet and Higher Education* 2 (1999): 87–105.

Garrison, D. Randy, Terry Anderson, and Walter Archer. "Critical Thinking, Cognitive Presence, and Computer Conferencing in Distance Education." *American Journal of Distance Education* 15, no. 1 (2001): 7–23.

Garrison, D. Randy, Terry Anderson, and Walter Archer. "A Theory of Critical Inquiry in Online Distance Education." In

M. G. Moore & W. G. Anderson (eds.), *Handbook of Distance Education*. Mahwah, NJ: Erlbaum, 2003. 113–127.

Garrison, D. Randy, Terry Anderson, and Walter Archer. "The First Decade of the Community of Inquiry Framework: A Retrospective." *The Internet and Higher Education* 13, no. 1–2 (2010): 5–9. dx.doi.org/10.1016/j.iheduc.2009.10.003.

Gonsalvez, Jennifer. "Frickin Packets." Cult of Pedagogy. Last modified March 26, 2018. cultofpedagogy.com/busysheets.

Guo, Philip J., Juho Kim, and Rob Rubin. "How Video Production Affects Student Engagement: An Empirical Study of MOOC Videos." In "Proceedings of the First ACM Conference on Learning@ Scale." March 2014. researchgate.net/publication/262393281_How_video_production_affects _student_engagement_An_empirical_study_of_MOOC_ videos.

Henderson, Michael, and Michael Phillips. "Video-Based Feedback on Student Assessment: Scarily Personal." *Australasian Journal of Educational Technology* 31, no. 1 (2015). doi.org/10.14742/ajet.1878.

Heritage, Margeret. *Formative Assessment: Making It Happen in the Classroom*. Thousand Oaks, CA: Corwin Press, 2010.

Horn, Michael B., and Heather Staker. *The Rise of K-12 Blended Learning*. Mountain View, CA: Innosight Institute, 2011.

IBM. "Enterprise Design Field Guide." Accessed March 8, 2021. ibm.com/cloud/architecture/files/design-thinking-field-guide.pdf.

Kabanoff, Boris. "Equity, Equality, Power, and Conflict." *Academy of Management Review* 16, no. 2 (1991): 416–441.

Kalb, Ben, and Rebecca Peters. Interview with Zaretta Hammond. *Vrain Waves*. Podcast. May 12, 2020. blogs.svvsd.org/vrainwaves/transcript-episode-056-apollo -13ing-it-with-zaretta-hammond.

Kilbane, Claire R., and Natalie Milman. *Teaching Models: Designing Instruction for 21st Century Learners*. Columbus, OH: Pearson Education, 2013.

Koca, Fatih. "Motivation to Learn and Teacher–Student Relationship." *Journal of International Education and Leadership* 6, no. 2 (2016): 1–20.

Korman, Hailly, Bonnie O'Keefe, and Matt Repka. "Missing in the Margins: Estimating the Scale of the COVID-19 Attendance Crisis." Last modified October 21, 2020. bellwethereducation.org/publication/missing -margins-estimating-scale-covid-19-attendance-crisis.

Mattarella-Micke, Andrew, and Sian Beilock. "Individual Differences in Working Memory: Implications for Learning and Performance." *Encyclopedia of the Sciences of Learning*, Boston: Springer, 2012. 498–501.

Matthews, Kelly, Victoria Andrews, and Peter Adams. "Social Learning Spaces and Student Engagement." *Higher Education Research & Development* 30, no. 2 (2011): 105–120.

McDonald, Joseph, Nancy Mohr, Alan Dichter, and Elaine McDonald. *The Power of Protocols: An Educator's Guide to Improving Practice*, 3rd ed. New York: Teachers College Press, 2013.

McTighe, Jay. "What Is a Performance Task? (Part 1). Defined Learning." Last modified April 10, 2015. Blog. performancetask.com/what-is-a-performance-task-part-1 -9fa0d99ead3b.

Meyer, Anne, David Rose, and David Gordon. *Universal Design for Learning: Theory and Practice.* Wakefield, MA: CAST Professional Publishing, 2014.

Mikel, Betsy. "How Brené Brown Runs Emotionally Intelligent Zoom Meetings." *Inc.* Accessed March 8, 2021. inc.com/ betsy-mikel/how-brene-brown-runs-emotionally-intelligen t-zoom-meetings.html.

New York Times. "75 years of crosswords." Last modified February 14, 2017. nytimes.com/interactive/2017/02/14/ crosswords/new-york-times-crossword-timeline.html.

Noguera, Pedro. "Where the Promise of the American Dream Falls Short in Schools." *Edutopia.* Last modified December 11, 2020. edutopia.org/video/ where-promise-american-dream-falls-short-schools.

Novak, Katie, and Kristan Rodriguez. *UDL Progression Rubric.* CAST Professional Publishing, 2018. castpublishing.org/wp-content/uploads/2018/02/UDL_Progression_Rubric_FINAL_Web_REV1.pdf.

Patrick, Susan, Kathryn Kennedy, and Allison Powell. *Mean What You Say: Defining and Integrating Personalized, Blended and Competency Education.* Vienna, VA: International Association for K–12 Online Learning, 2013.

Powell, Allison, Beth Rabbit, and Kathryn Kennedy. *iNACOL Blended Learning Teacher Competency Framework.* Vienna, VA: International Association for K-12 Online Learning, 2014.

Rahman, Saemah, Zuria Mahmud, Siti Fatimah Mohd Yassin, Ruslin Amir, and Khadijah Wan Ilias. "The Development of Expert Learners in the Classroom." *Contemporary Issues in Education Research (CIER)* 3, no. 1 (2010).

Rao, Kavita, and Grace Meo. "Using Universal Design for Learning to Design Standards-Based Lessons." *SAGE Open* 6, no. 4 (2016): 1–12.

Salend, Spencer J. *Creating inclusive classrooms: Effective, Differentiated, and Reflective Practices.* Columbus, OH: Pearson Education, 2016.

Schlechty, Phillip. *Engaging Students: The Next Level of Working on the Work.* San Francisco: Jossey-Bass, 2011.

Shabani, Karim, Mohamad Khatib, and Saman Ebadi. "Vygotsky's Zone of Proximal Development: Instructional Implications and Teachers' Professional Development." *English Language Teaching* 3, no. 4 (2010): 237–248.

Sinek, Simon. *Start with Why.* London: Penguin Books, 2011.

Staker, Heather, and Michael Horn. *Classifying K-12 Blended Learning.* Mountain View, CA: Innosight Institute, 2012. Accessed March 8, 2020. christenseninstitute.org/wp-content/uploads/2013/04/Classifying-K-12-blended-learning.pdf.

Sung, Ki. "What the Shortcomings of EdTech Mean for Improving Distance Learning and Schools," *Mindshift.*

September 25, 2020. kqed.org/mindshift/56694/
what-the-shortcomings-of-edtech-mean-for-improving
-distance-learning-and-schools.

Swan, Karen. "Social Construction of Knowledge and the
Community of Inquiry Framework." In *Open and Distance
Education Theory Revisited: Implications for a Digital Era*,
edited by I. Jung. Tokyo: Springer Briefs in Education, 2019.

Tawfik, Andrew, Woei Hung, and Phillipe Giabbeanelli.
"Comparing Different Inquiry-Based Approaches."
Interdisciplinary Journal of Problem-based Learning 14, no.
1 (2020).

The New Teacher Project (TNTP). "The Opportunity Myth:
What Students Can Show Us about How School Is Letting
Them Down—and How to Fix It." Accessed March 8,
2020. opportunitymyth.tntp.org/.

Thibodeau, Thomas. "UDL, Online Accessibility, and Virtual
Reality: Designing Accessible and Engaging Online Courses."
In *Transforming Higher Education through Universal Design
for Learning: An International Perspective*, edited by Sean
Bracken and Katie Novak. London: Routledge, Taylor and
Francis Group, 2019.

Tomlinson, Carol. *The Differentiated Classroom: Responding to the
Needs of All Learners.* Alexandria, VA: ASCD, 2000.

Tran, Khoa, Phuong Nguyen, Thao Dang, Tran Ton. "The
Impacts of the High-Quality Workplace Relationships on Job
Performance: A Perspective on Staff Nurses in Vietnam."
Behavioral Sciences 8, no. 12 (2018): 109.

Tucker, Catlin, Tiffany Wycoff, and Jason Green. *Blended
Learning in Action: A Practical Guide toward Sustainable
Change.* Thousand Oaks, CA: Sage Publications, 2017.

Tucker, Catlin. *Balance with Blended Learning: Partner with
Your Students to Reimagine Learning and Reclaim Your Life.*
Thousand Oaks, CA: Sage Publications, 2020.

Valdez, Amber, Sola Takahashi, Kelsey Krausen, Alicia Bowman,
and Edith Gurrola. *Getting Better at Getting More Equitable:
Opportunities and Barriers for Using Continuous Improvement
to Advance Educational Equity.* WestEd, 2020.

Wang, Margaret, Geneva Haertel, and Herbert Walberg. "The Effectiveness of Collaborative School-Linked Services." National Research Center on Education in the Inner Cities. 93(5e) (1993).

Walden Woods Project. "Myths and Misconceptions." Last accessed March 9, 2021. walden.org/education/for -students/myths-and-misconceptions/.

Wenger, Etienne. "Communities of Practice and Social Learning Systems: The Career of a Concept." In *Social Learning Systems and Communities of Practice*. London: Springer, 2010, 179–198.

Wenger, Etienne. *Communities of Practice: A Brief Introduction*. Accessed March 8, 2021. scholarsbank.uoregon.edu/ xmlui/bitstream/handle/1794/11736/A percent20brief percent20introduction percent20to percent20CoP.pdf.

Wenger, Etienne, Richard McDermott, and William M. Snyder. *Cultivating Communities of Practice: A guide to Managing Knowledge.* Cambridge, MA: Harvard Business Press, 2002.

Buck Institute for Education. "What is PBL?" Last accessed March 8, 2021. pblworks.org/what-is-pbl.

Wiggins, Grant, and Jay McTighe. *Understanding by Design*, 2nd edition. Alexandria, VA: ASCD, 2005.

Yazzie-Mintz, Ethan. *Charting the Path from Engagement to Achievement: A Report on the 2009 High School Survey of Student Engagement.* Bloomington, IN: Center for Evaluation and Education Policy, 2009.

Yilmaz, Fatma, Gizem Karaoglan, and Hafize Keser. "The Impact of Reflective Thinking Activities in E-learning: A Critical Review of the Empirical Research." *Computers & Education* 95 (2016): 163–173.

Acknowledgments

From Katie

Catlin: I'm elated we met and are planning to run off to a deserted island to write more books! It has been such a joy to work with you. Learning more about blended learning has challenged everything I know about design, and I love that. I will always be a better educator because of you. No doubt, there is more collaboration (and sparkling golden tans) in our future. You are a brilliant woman, and I can't wait until we can celebrate this book in person.

George: I am the little sister you never wanted, but can't live without! Like all good little sisters, I am a constant nudge and provide endless entertainment with my story-telling and jokes. Remember the one about the bird, the cigar, and the rock? Best. Joke. Ever. In all seriousness, I am so grateful for you for always believing in me, pushing me to learn more, and connecting me with amazing, brilliant people like Catlin. Much love!

To the team at IMPress and Reading List Editorial: You have been fabulous to work with. Even though Catlin and I were a little nervous to leave APA formatting behind, we now embrace *Chicago*. (Note: Thank goodness for copy editors!)

To my framily: You know who you are. I couldn't have gotten through the last year and a half without all of you. I have the slideshow to prove it! This life takes a village, and I am so blessed that I have found mine.

Lon: As my mom and dad always say to each other, "If I could do this whole thing again, I would choose you every time." Same.

And Torin, Aylin, Brecan, and Boden: You are the best part of every day, and being your momma is my greatest joy. I love getting to share this beautiful life with all of you—even when you refer to me as "Booter McTooter," which is ridiculous. (;

From Catlin

Katie: For years I have known there was a synergy between UDL and blended learning. I felt the same synergy working with you! You are a gifted storyteller. Your powerful and entertaining anecdotes challenged me to grow as a writer. I also developed as a learner through this process, benefiting from your knowledge and expertise! I, too, look forward to celebrating this book in person. Maybe we can toast our accomplishment with martinis in hand and red stilettos on our feet while enjoying a duck boat tour the next time I'm in Boston!

George: Thank you for connecting me with Katie! Working with her has been a highlight of my career, and it would not have been possible without you.

IMPress and Reading List Editorial teams: Writing a book is a daunting and wonderfully exhausting process. You made it easier every step of the way. Thank you!

Cheyenne and Maddox: You light me up and inspire my work in education. When I imagine the experience I want *all* kids to have in school, I'm thinking of you and what I would want for you as learners. I love you to the moon and back!

Erin: This year has been hard on so many fronts, and through it all you were there. I'm beyond grateful to have you as my sister walking through this life. Thank you for making this dark year brighter by bringing Cash into the world. I adore our little Cashew Nut!

Sara: Our trip to Ireland was the beginning of a series of happy accidents that led me to a career in education. This work has brought me so much joy and fulfillment, but I don't think it would have happened without your carefree spirit enticing me on an adventure that would change the course of my life. Your friendship is one of the great gifts in my life.

About the Authors

KATIE NOVAK, ED.D., is an internationally renowned education consultant, best-selling author, graduate instructor at UPenn, and a former assistant superintendent of schools in Massachusetts. With nineteen years of experience in teaching and administration and an earned doctorate in curriculum and teaching, Katie designs and  presents workshops both nationally and internationally that focus on the implementation of inclusive practices, Universal Design for Learning (UDL), multi-tiered systems of support, and universally designed leadership. Novak's work has impacted educators worldwide as her contributions and collaborations have built upon the foundation for an educational framework that is critical for student success.

Dr. Novak is the author of eight books, including *UDL Now! A Teacher's Guide to Applying Universal Design for Learning in Today's Classrooms, Innovate Inside the Box* with George Couros, and *Equity by Design* with Mirko Chardin. Her work has been highlighted in many publications, including *Edutopia*, Cult of Pedagogy, *Language, Principal, ADDitude, Commonwealth*, the *Huffington Post, Principal Leadership, District Administration, ASCD Education Update*, and *School Administrator*.

DR. CATLIN TUCKER is a bestselling author, international trainer, and keynote speaker. She was named Teacher of the Year in 2010 in Sonoma County, where she taught for sixteen years. Catlin earned her doctorate in learning technologies from Pepperdine University, where she researched teacher engagement in blended learning environments.

Catlin works with districts, schools, and teachers shifting to blended learning. Catlin designs and facilitates professional learning to help leaders and teachers cultivate a mindset, skill set, and toolset necessary to thrive in blended learning environments. Catlin encourages educators to blend the best aspects of technology and tradition to shift students to the center of learning. She also works with leadership teams to explore how they can support this shift by developing a robust professional learning infrastructure that weaves professional learning into the fabric of the school.

Dr. Tucker is a professor in the Masters of Arts in Teaching program at Pepperdine University and has written a series of bestselling books on blended learning, which include *Balance With Blended Learning, Blended Learning in Action, Power Up Blended Learning*, and *Blended Learning in Grades 4-12*. She is active on Twitter (@Catlin_Tucker) and writes an internationally ranked blog at CatlinTucker.com.

Speaking

Katie Novak

Katie Novak collaborates with schools and organizations to design and deliver high-quality, evidence-based professional development focused on Universal Design for Learning (UDL) and multitiered systems of support (MTSS). Through innovative, flexible, and engaging practices (like a professional DJ in all live virtual sessions!), Katie provides keynote presentations and in-person and virtual workshops to educators around the world who believe, without exception, that all means all. Whether you have a group of five or five thousand, need in-person or online assistance, Novak and associates will deliver professional development to excite and engage your team.

FOR MORE INFORMATION, VISIT
NOVAKEDUCATION.COM

Dr. Catlin Tucker

Dr. Catlin Tucker designs and facilitates learning experiences to support leaders, coaches, and teachers in the shift to blended learning. Catlin customizes her keynotes, training sessions, and workshops to target the specific needs of each group. Catlin's workshops—virtual and in-person—are grounded in discussion, practice, and hands-on application. Catlin helps educators develop a growth mindset, flexible skill set, and robust toolset that will allow them to navigate any teaching and learning landscape with confidence. Catlin wants educators to understand and harness the power of blended learning to remove barriers, personalize learning, and develop dynamic learning communities capable of making meaning. The goal is to shift students to the center of learning, where they belong!

Catlin can deliver a keynote to inspire your teachers if you are just getting started. She can facilitate engaging workshops designed to guide leaders in a visioning process, coaches through a blended learning coaching cycle, or teachers in designing and facilitating learning using the various blended learning models. She can even offer coaching sessions to support implementation. No matter where you are in your blended learning journey, Catlin can support your continued growth and progress.

FOR MORE INFORMATION, VISIT
CATLINTUCKER.COM

MORE FROM

Impressbooks.org

Empower
What Happens When Students Own Their Learning
by A.J. Juliani and John Spencer

Learner-Centered Innovation
Spark Curiosity, Ignite Passion, and Unleash Genius
by Katie Martin

Unleash Talent
Bringing Out the Best in Yourself and the Learners You Serve
by Kara Knollmeyer

Reclaiming Our Calling
Hold On to the Heart, Mind, and Hope of Education
by Brad Gustafson

Take the L.E.A.P.
Ignite a Culture of Innovation
by Elisabeth Bostwick

Drawn to Teach
An Illustrated Guide to Transforming Your Teaching written
by Josh Stumpenhorst and illustrated by Trevor Guthke

Math Recess
Playful Learning in an Age of Disruption
by Sunil Singh and Dr. Christopher Brownell

Innovate Inside the Box
Empowering Learners Through UDL and Innovator's Mindset
by George Couros and Katie Novak

Personal & Authentic
Designing Learning Experiences that Last a Lifetime
by Thomas C. Murray

Learner-Centered Leadership
A Blueprint for Transformational Change in
Learning Communities
by Devin Vodicka

Kids These Days
A Game Plan For (Re)Connecting With Those We
Teach, Lead, & Love
by Dr. Jody Carrington